Y0-BZJ-959

Dear Marlene,
All the Best!
Maili Nung

PRAISE FOR SMART RISK

"Smart Risk *will challenge the fundamentals of your financial decision-making process. A must-read for all investors!"*

—Victor G. Dodig, president and CEO, *CIBC*

"You have achieved a great measure of success, yet you've remembered the stepping-stones along the way, including your grandfather, father, and the rungs of the ladder you have climbed. You are inspiring."

—Joseph Segal, president, *Kingswood Capital Corporation*

"How do we ensure our financial well being through a significantly extended period of retirement? Whether you are an advisor, an individual investor, or just someone trying to figure out how to navigate our evolving world, you will find Smart Risk *a very helpful resource."*

—Warren Collier, CEO, *iShares Canada*

"Maili's story is a metaphor for the power of intelligence, education, thoughtful analysis, perseverance, and grace—in short, a roadmap for the right way forward in personal investment, high finance, or any other endeavour in business or life. I commend the author and recommend it to you."

—Robert Helsley, dean, *Sauder School of Business*; Grosvenor Professor of Cities, Business Economics and Public Policy

"Maili Wong brings one of the best perspectives in managing wealth for individuals, with deep experiences, which have shaped her overall process. Smart Risk *has a clear and direct message on what really matters for all Canadians in managing their money and meeting their long-term goals."*

—Som Seif, president and CEO, *Purpose Investments Inc.*

"Highly readable and full of common-sense financial-planning advice, Smart Risk *uses real-life investment case studies to identify and assess common fears, mistakes, and concerns of investors and then explains how to analyze and best resolve these issues to maximize personal financial goals."*

—Andrew McCreath, markets commentator, *Business News Network (BNN-TV)*; CEO and chief investment officer, *Forge First Asset Management*

"Maili Wong has taken a topic that is increasingly complex and created a smart, thorough, and effective framework to deal with the aspirations and challenges Canadian investors face daily. Timely and driven by her passion for life—a powerful combination!"

—Barry Gordon, president and CEO, *First Asset*

"Maili carefully unpacks financial markets theory into smart doses of investment wisdom. She offers the reader a fine balance between tactical and strategic approaches to managing risk and building wealth over time. An excellent guide for the novice to informed investor."

—Satya Pradhuman, director of research, *Cirrus Research LLC*, New York

"The best investment books are almost always written from the mind and from the heart. Maili has brought her conviction and process to these pages with a deft touch that I am sure many Canadians will understand and enjoy. There are very few in our investment world who have experienced what Maili has and certainly none that have done it with such skill and success."

—Ben Cheng, president and chief investment officer, *Aston Hill Asset Management*

"Being able to overcome the emotional attachment to our money decisions and see opportunity in the fog of immediate uncertainty is an important life skill that Maili understands and masters. Smart Risk *will help you with your plan toward living the work- optional life."*

—Larry Berman, television host, *Berman's Call, Business News Network (BNN)*; cofounder, *ETF Capital Management* and *The Independent Investor Institute*

"Smart Risk *is the greatest investment one could make in personal growth and needs to be in the hands of all families. I believe the wisdom Maili has shared will positively impact the lives of families globally."*

—Candy Ho, vice president *Element Lifestyle Retirement Inc.*

"Maili Wong's Smart Risk *is an invaluable resource for anyone who aspires to make well-informed decisions about achieving their lifelong financial goals."*

—Gayla DeHart, PhD, cofounder, *Live Well Exercise Clinics*

"Maili has written a treasure of a book, filled with practical advice on how to live a Smart Risk life. By sharing her personal story of resilience as a survivor of 9/11 in New York, Maili empowers the reader to find their courage and desire to pursue their dreams."

—Francesco Lombardo, FEA, managing director, *Veritage Family Office*; author, *Entitled Brat or Contributing Leader? Which One Are You … Are You Sure?* and *Great White Elephant: Why Rich Kids Hate Their Parents!*

"Smart Risk *is a smart read for investors of all ages. Maili's gift is her ability to reframe fear so readers can face life's difficult moments and not be paralyzed by it. She offers optimism and resilience in its place, inviting readers to take smart risks and change the course of their lives so that it is filled with purpose, meaning, and peace of mind."*

—Debbie Gilbert, certified professional consultant on aging; founder, *Generations*

"Maili Wong's Smart Risk *captures the essence of what it means to think differently and then act differently, in order to blaze a path toward achieving one's financial vision of success. Bravo, Maili!"*

—John DeHart, cofounder, *Nurse Next Door*

"Smart Risk *uses real-life examples from her clients to let the reader know that the right strategy can get any investor to their desired goal and provides insight into proven investment strategies that Maili developed working amongst the best and the brightest investors on Wall Street."*

—Trevor Bruno, president, *Intrawest Resort*

"Smart Risk *breaks down what is often the daunting task of financial and investment planning into a clear and easy-to-understand model. This book is practical, easy to read, and sprinkled with heart-warming stories and lessons from Maili's personal life. If you look forward to a work-optional life, this is your playbook!*"

—Wendy Sage-Hayward, MA, FEA,
The Family Business Consulting Group

"Smart Risk *is full of practical, actionable, wealth-building ideas shared through the power of storytelling. I recommend this book to both men and women who are looking for a new way to approach retirement and a work-optional life.*

—Kelley Keehn, personal finance expert; award-winning author of nine books, including *Protecting You and Your Money: A Guide to Avoiding Identity Theft and Fraud*

"*Maili's* Smart Risk *approach shows the way to a healthier relationship with your investment advisor ... and a stronger portfolio. Read it and make the shifts to Smart Risk.*"

—Anne C. Graham, profit and growth accelerator;
author of the #1 best seller *Profit in Plain Sight: The Proven Leadership Path to Unlock Profit, Passion, and Growth*

"Smart Risk *is an engaging and practical book written for investors who are motivated to strategically grow their wealth. Without doubt, Maili is very well equipped to lead multigenerational families to adopt a smart risk approach to investing. Maili gives readers the opportunity to get to know her and to consider the importance of resilience, trust, and clarity when building financial security."*

—Michèle Soregaroli, founder and coach,
Transformation Catalyst Corp.

"Maili takes you through a journey that is engaging, will educate you to make better financial decisions, and will inspire you to take charge of your financial affairs. Smart Risk *is a must-read for any savvy investor."*

—Renato Cavaliere, CEO, *Canadian Safe-step Tubs Inc.*

"Maili Wong demystifies investing in Smart Risk *and, through real-life anecdotes, guides readers down the path to a "Work-Optional Lifestyle."*

—Shana Hennigan, managing director,
Promontory Interfinancial Network, New York

"Risk is the nameless fear too many financial professionals fail to talk about. Maili clearly explains how you don't have to leave the management of risk to the hands of fate in Smart Risk."

—Brad Simpson, founder, *Alt Strategist*

"From debunking the myths of investing to the "5 Ps" of her Smart Risk Investing Roadmap, Maili Wong provides an easily digestible, approachable method to achieving the work-optional life."

—Dawn Schooler, MA, FEA, principal,
Family Enterprise Consulting Inc.

"If you want to understand what is possible when professional advice is collaborative, intelligent, accountable, and sincere, read this book and your expectations of financial advice will gain a new dimension. Maili Wong is the quintessential financial professional, a trusted confidant who combines sophisticated, proven investment strategies for portfolio management with her strong personal commitment to help her clients achieve their lifelong ambitions and needs."

—James Pelmore, FEA, director,
Private Client Group, HollisWealth, Scotia Capital Inc.;
managing partner, *Clearplan Insurance Advisors Inc.*

"Smart Risk *is a smart choice for people who want to take an enlightened view to managing their wealth and the opportunities to enjoy a purposeful life. Maili Wong's book provides a wealth of insight, shared experience, and heart-warming stories of people who have transcended the complex world of finance and developed a meaningful path to managing their money rather than being managed by it. Written in an easy conversational, yet informative style, Smart Risk is well worth the time and energy of anyone wanting to change their lives for the better."*

—Duncan L Sinclair, MA, CPA, CA, ICD.D, FEA, vice chair,
DELOITTE Canada

"Maili Wong's Smart Risk *is the smart choice for any person or family attempting to look over the horizon at their financial future. She presents a roadmap, like a seasoned commander issuing a pre-battle order, yet the book is personal and filled with warm stories and clear, concise, practical applications."*

—Art Gorman, financial advisor, *Wells Fargo Advisors* in New York City; former chief operating officer, *Municipal Markets / Public Finance at Bank of America / Merrill Lynch* in New York

SMART RISK

SMART RISK

INVEST LIKE THE *wealthy*
TO ACHIEVE A *work-optional life*

MAILI WONG, CFA

Copyright © 2016 by Maili Wong, CFA

All rights reserved. No part of this book may be used or reproduced in any manner whatsoever without prior written consent of the author, except as provided by the United States of America copyright law.

Published by Advantage, Charleston, South Carolina.
Member of Advantage Media Group.

ADVANTAGE is a registered trademark and the Advantage colophon is a trademark of Advantage Media Group, Inc.

Printed in the United States of America.

ISBN: 978-1-59932-602-3
LCCN: 2015959126

10 9 8 7 6 5 4 3 2

This publication is designed to provide accurate and authoritative information in regard to the subject matter covered. It is sold with the understanding that the publisher is not engaged in rendering legal, accounting, or other professional services. If legal advice or other expert assistance is required, the services of a competent professional person should be sought.

The content of this book is not intended to constitute legal, accounting, financial, or tax advice. If you would like personalized financial advice please contact a licensed financial professional in your jurisdiction. The views expressed in this book are the views of the author in her personal capacity and do not represent those of her employer.

Advantage Media Group is proud to be a part of the Tree Neutral® program. Tree Neutral offsets the number of trees consumed in the production and printing of this book by taking proactive steps such as planting trees in direct proportion to the number of trees used to print books. To learn more about Tree Neutral, please visit **www.treeneutral.com**. To learn more about Advantage's commitment to being a responsible steward of the environment, please visit **www.advantagefamily.com/green**

Advantage Media Group is a publisher of business, self-improvement, and professional development books and online learning. We help entrepreneurs, business leaders, and professionals share their Stories, Passion, and Knowledge to help others Learn & Grow. Do you have a manuscript or book idea that you would like us to consider for publishing? Please visit **advantagefamily.com** or call **1.866.775.1696.**

Stories of Empowerment and Freedom Found in the Most Unlikely Places: The Uncertain World of Risk

To my mom and dad,
for teaching me that anything is possible.
To my husband, Keith, for making everything possible.

ACKNOWLEDGMENTS

First, I wish to thank all of my wonderful clients for being my inspiration to write this book. I thank you for sharing your stories, your fears, your passions, and your heartfelt dreams with me over the years. I am grateful for the trust you have placed in me and my team. You are a constant motivator for me to work harder and smarter every day. Please note, that while many of you generously allowed us to use your stories, we changed your names and a few facts to protect your anonymity or amalgamated some of your experiences to highlight themes we see when working to achieve your goals. A special thanks to Dr. Lloyd Baron for writing the foreword and to the many others who agreed to share their stories in this book.

To the publishing and editorial team at Advantage Media, particularly Scott Neville, George Stevens, and Adam Witty: thank you for believing in me and being so committed to making this book a success. Especially to my editor Kathryn Fallon: your nearly two decades of experience at *Time* and genuine passion for my stories and message were the catalysts I needed to take on this challenge.

To my team at The Wong Group, especially Cindy Liang, Icy Chiu, Elaine Lee, Gabriel Chua, and my dad, Terry: thank you for being the best team I have ever worked with and for the focus, dedication, and strength you bring every day so we can deliver complete confidence in our service and performance to our clients.

To the management group at CIBC Wood Gundy, especially Greg Johnson, Gary Whitfield, Grace McSorley, Jonathan Carter,

Monique Gravel, Steve Geist, and Victor Dodig: thank you for your continuous support and willingness to take a Smart Risk with me.

To my team at Noodle Wave, especially Roy Chong and Audrey Kwan, and to Brand Velocity, particularly Kelley Keehn and Wyatt Cavanaugh: thank you for sharing your creative brilliance to push me beyond my comfort zone and for helping me develop this book project into an interactive media experience.

To my mentors, coaches, and friends, especially Shana Hennigan, Michele Soregaroli, Lindsay Chan, and Ron Huntington: thank you for enduring my endless questions and for all of your honest and constructive feedback and ideas.

To Mom and Dad: you have given me more than life; you have shown me the meaning of unconditional love. You've been my best friends, my inspiration, and the first people I consult for a valued opinion. I've always been able to count on you and will be forever grateful.

To Keith: thank you for being my rock, my number-one supporter and life partner. You pick me up when I fall and always have my back. You are everything to me.

To my children, Jaayda and Maxwell: you two are my golden rays of sunlight. Thank you for reminding me every day of my life's greater purpose and inspiring me to create an exponential impact beyond myself.

To you, the reader: thank you for inviting me into your journey. I hope this book creates value for you and your loved ones.

TABLE OF CONTENTS

FOREWORD

It is not the strongest of species that survives, nor the most intelligent, but the one most responsive to change.

Purposeful Darwinism

All those who have engaged an investment advisor or broker to manage their portfolio may find this story familiar: It is just past the New Year festivities, and it is time for your annual review of the performance of your stocks and bonds. Unfortunately, the news is not good; your expectations have not been met. Your advisor doesn't help the situation by telling you that even though your returns may not be stellar, a series of indices performed even worse.

What to do? You sense that you should find another broker, but the relationship has become personal and you don't want to move precipitously. Results for the next year are promised to improve. You sense that there must be a better way, but you do not know how to find it. At the same time, you need a plan to start defining just how much you want to work in your not-too-distant future. However, to get there, you must have the certainty that your portfolio will grow as you had projected. What you need is a better way to select, reward, and terminate the person to whom you have given control over your financial destiny.

I turned to the corporate world to find my model. One of the most successful global technology companies, Amazon, is reputed to have one of the industry's most demanding cycles of constantly hiring new employees, driving them hard, and then cutting employee numbers. The company, founded and run by Jeff Bezos, rejects many of the popular management bromides that other corporations at least pay lip service to and has, instead, designed what many workers call Purposeful Darwinism. The company keeps the stars by offering a combination of incredible opportunities and outstanding compensation; at the same time, the least performers leave or are fired in an annual systematic culling. Maybe a variation of this model would work in constructing a relationship with my professional advisors.

Another, more local, example of this successful approach has been demonstrated by an entrepreneur who has risen to the ranks of the Forbes World's Billionaires list. Jimmy Pattison, self-made businessman and founder, chairman, and CEO of the Jim Pattison Group and still active into his eighties, has amassed a multibillion-dollar fortune from a diversified conglomeration of corporations. During his early days while he was growing his car dealerships, he allegedly fired, at the end of every month, the salesman with the poorest sales record, while rewarding his best. His path to success also inspired me to adjust my stagnant advisory relationships.

Thus, years ago, as I engaged in my version of Purposeful Darwinism, I decided to select highly recommended investment advisors and invest a modest sum of money. If they were successful at the end of the year, the amount they had under their control was doubled. Conversely, if a particular broker had the worst performance for two consecutive years, that broker's portion of my portfolio was collapsed and the broker was politely told that I was moving on. At times, I had as many as six brokers with disparate strategies commanding various parts of my assets, all competing against each other to do their best and most certainly, at least, to not find themselves at the bottom of the heap. During this process, I was introduced to Maili Wong.

Maili had just returned from New York to join her father's wealth management practice and I, following a glowing recommendation from a banker, had just begun to invest with The Wong Group. Right from the start, I was impressed. Maili's analysis was crisp and thorough, and her connections in New York and Toronto were current and strategic. We began to work together in 2006, but it was during the major financial crash of 2007–2008 that her brilliance and uniqueness in the Vancouver investment community was truly demonstrated through her creation of the Smart Risk strategy.

From the crash to this very day, there has been a consistent theme in the investment environment: the world will not revert to some past norm, and the speed at which change will be experienced will continue to accelerate. Whatever investment strategy you used formerly is no longer valid. Whatever risk profile you formerly assumed directed your investment allocations is now open to review.

Yesterday's risk-sheltered investments have, in the current environment, been transformed into investments most exposed to uncertainty and possible loss. In order to succeed in today's investment environment, because situations change so rapidly, everyone needs a strategy that keeps decision making separate from an often-flawed emotional response network. Given the breadth of change and volatility we are experiencing, investors today need advisors who challenge the orthodox assumptions and modify approaches to fit the realities and exigencies of the environment.

Once, I had six investment brokers; now I have only one. It is not for the lack of adequate contenders; rather, it is because Maili has consistently out performed the field. She is that good.

Lloyd I. Baron, PhD, Economics

PART ONE

Resilience: What Is Needed to Overcome Challenges to Building Wealth Today

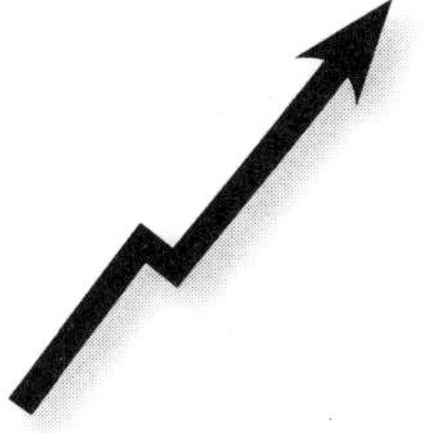

CHAPTER 1

A Winning Strategy of Resilience

Chance favors the prepared mind.
—Louis Pasteur

A lesson in rejecting the safe choice

Back in the 1970s, a young woman was preparing for her first trip overseas with her husband. She had just gotten all of the required live vaccinations to go to China. Suddenly, she started feeling sick to her stomach.

So she went to see her doctor, and she was shocked to find out that she was pregnant. As the blood rushed from her face, she thought, *What now?* They hadn't been planning for children yet, and they were about to leave on this extended trip throughout rural China for six to eight weeks. And then her doctor dropped the bomb: "You may want to consider having an abortion because the series of live vaccinations that you just took could put the baby at risk."

That's when Cindy realized the gravity of her choice. So that evening she told her husband the news and what the doctor had advised. They decided to seek a second opinion. That evening she had a dream, and in it, her grandfather, who had been deceased for many years but with whom she had shared a special bond, visited her. He held Cindy in his arms, and he whispered in her ear, "Cindy, everything is going to be all right."

She woke up with a start and couldn't go back to sleep. That next day, she went to visit another physician who specialized in immunology and who took great care and time to understand her situation. The specialist, while agreeing with the first doctor's assessment that the baby might have severe deformities as a result of the live vaccinations, said there was also the chance the baby could be completely normal. The specialist told Cindy there was still a good chance the baby could be fine and a wonderful blessing for her and her family.

That's when Cindy's mind-set shifted. She recognized that the safe choice would have been to end the pregnancy, but then she found the strength and the courage to take the risk and step across the chasm to the other side. Cindy decided to have the baby. Throughout its early journey in utero, this little baby fought to survive against the odds. I am glad Cindy made this decision to have the baby because, eight months later, she gave birth to me.

My existence is thanks to my mother's courage to take an educated and informed chance on me. In the short term, the right decision might have appeared to be the safe choice to avoid the painful chance of deformities or complications. But often, the better choice means stepping out of the safety zone to take a *good* risk—a *Smart Risk.*

A challenge to you, the reader

Have you ever been faced with a difficult decision and felt compelled to take the safe path out of fear or the path of least resistance to avoid pain? How about in a financial situation? Why did you choose the safe path, and what was the result? What were you afraid of, and what were you hoping to achieve?

What if there was a way for you to put yourself in a place of financial security and strength? What if there was an investment strategy that actually adapts to the changing environment, helping you truly achieve financial freedom sooner through a sustainable source of income for life?

For the past fifteen years, I've had the privilege of working with brilliant investors, business owners, and professionals from all over the world. Gleaning techniques from ultra-wealthy and successful investors, I help clients build better lives using the art and science of wealth creation so they can enjoy an active retirement sooner. I help them design and follow their own roadmap to a Work-Optional Life.

The goal of this book is to offer insights and solutions used by some of the wealthiest and most successful investors to empower everyday people to make better and more informed financial decisions so they can achieve active retirement sooner. People today need more than knowledge; they need a clear roadmap enabling them to make better choices for a financially secure future. This book is your opportunity to map your path to financial resiliency, accelerate wealth building, and achieve your lifestyle goals.

Roots of success

I was born in Vancouver, British Columbia, and raised in the suburb of Burnaby. From a young age I've always been interested in business, but it was my father who recognized some of these characteristics in me. He had been in business for many years, and he was one of the early influencers in my life.

Growing up, I learned to respect the value of hard work, seeing my father work long hours and my mother give up her career to stay at home to raise my little brother, Christopher, and me. At an early age, I took to academics, particularly reading and math, and my teachers tried pushing me into special programmes for "gifted" children, but I refused to attend, preferring to play with my friends and do "normal" things. I enjoyed sports, dancing, music, art, and science. On school holidays, my dad would bring me into his office so that I could see what it was like to have a real job. I was six years old, and he would drag me, at 6 a.m., into the office where he was a successful financial advisor. I would answer his phones, collect trade tickets, and try not to fall asleep at his desk.

Around age seven, I took up piano lessons, and while my brother was the one who originally wanted to learn, I really enjoyed and continued to pursue it all the way up to the Royal Conservatory's highest designation of ARCT (Associate of the Royal Conservatory of Music). By the age of thirteen, I realized that if I wanted to go to the movies with friends or buy new clothes, I would need to earn spending money. I decided that teaching piano might be a good way to earn some income. So instead of babysitting, which I also did for a time, I focused on building a small piano teaching business.

At first, I took on four young students in the neighborhood. After budgeting the cost of books, stickers, and how much I'd have to earn to make the business profitable, I realized I could make about five times as much per hour teaching piano compared to what I could make working at the mall—but I was too young to work at the mall anyway.

By the time I reached high school, I started to think about the end game and what I wanted to achieve. I wanted to get into a good university. In my culture and my family, education is a high priority. As I entered grade 8 at Alpha Secondary School, I started thinking about ways to maximize the scholarships that I could earn to pay for university down the road, and from that day, that notion directed how I would spend my time, the grades I would need, and which student activities I'd need to join.

I joined sports teams, got elected to the student council, maintained a straight-A average, and ended up being in a good position to select from my choice of universities. With all the various scholarships I had earned, I was able to pay for my entire university education, plus books and other incidentals. My parents never had to pay for my education, and I never expected that they would. My parents supported me in many ways, but I always felt it was my own responsibility to work hard and not waste the opportunities I was grateful to have.

My studies at the University of British Columbia (UBC) gave me the chance to expand my horizons. I had initially planned on going into the medical field. However, my father suggested I consider some business courses. I was really interested in the sciences, but since I needed electives, I took a few business courses too. And to my surprise, it was in those business and economics classes where things got very interesting.

The calling

I was introduced to a unique finance programme at the University of British Columbia, called Portfolio Management Foundation (PMF). It had been created by a man who became one of my mentors, the late Milton Wong (no relation). Milton was a visionary who was a success in business and philanthropy. He wanted to create a programme at the university for students to learn how to manage money in a practical way, rather than just studying academic theory. Six students from the finance department were hand-selected each year to manage a multimillion-dollar university endowment portfolio.

It was a $3 million portfolio of real money, and it was completely run by the students. Remarkably, this portfolio has consistently outperformed its benchmark by a wide margin. According to Professor Robert Heinkel, the faculty advisor who has fostered the continued success of this programme, the PMF portfolio out performed the S&P/TSX Canadian Equity Index by 3.4 percent per year for the past twenty-five years.[1]

Out of hundreds of applicants, I was lucky enough to be selected for this mastermind group. My participation in the PMF changed the course of my life and propelled me along the road to financial services. It was the first time I truly felt I had a calling in the business world—as if someone were showing me I was destined for something in the investment industry. Sitting in our first PMF meeting, I realized how much I didn't know, and it was humbling. But it also

1 Source: University of British Columbia Portfolio Management Foundation

stirred my curiosity and challenged me to devour information in an attempt to figure out everything.

This PMF programme had a group of mentors whose mission was to educate students about real-life methods to manage money, as opposed to just the theory learned in textbooks. Our seasoned mentors taught us practical lessons about investing and encouraged us to think independently and avoid following the crowd, to critically analyze the underlying financial fundamentals of every potential investment, and to never be afraid to ask thoughtful questions.

I became a fund manager in 2000, the same year that Nortel Networks, a high-flying Canadian technology company, was worth more than 30 percent of the Canadian investment benchmark. To put that into perspective, this single company, which had yet to produce a dollar of profit, was worth more than three times the value of the top five Canadian banks combined.

It also meant that almost every mutual fund that tracked the Canadian market owned around 30 percent of the portfolio of that stock. Using the principles that we had learned from our mentors, we didn't own any Nortel shares at all. It was a difficult period for us because we had to stand accountable in front of an esteemed group of clients—community members, our board—every two months and defend our reasons why we didn't own any of this company, which at the time was a "high flyer." In that process, we had to reassess, think critically, and be able to defend our position. We also had to be open to the idea that we were wrong and take a view that wasn't short-term.

That was a turning point for me because a few months later, what became known as the tech bubble burst, and Nortel Networks, along with many other big, well-known Canadian and US bellwethers, dropped dramatically. Our decision had proven right. We were vindicated in the following year as Nortel shares plummeted from $124 per share in September 2000 to $0.47 per share in August 2002, and we had owned none in the portfolio. Most importantly, it was a huge learning experience—a life lesson: not to follow the herd but to think and act independently. From then on I was hooked.

From the med track to the finance track

Now a full-time finance student and portfolio manager for the PMF programme, I continued to work hard to learn more and hone my investment skills, while doing my best to balance academics and volunteer commitments. One of the big Wall Street firms, having heard about this PMF programme, decided to fly out and interview a few of us for a summer internship. The interviews were intense and intimidating, but I got the job. So at the age of twenty, I moved to New York for a summer internship at Merrill Lynch's headquarters.

I did a rotation across multiple areas including options and derivatives, trading, and debt capital markets. It was quite a life experience, being in New York and away from Vancouver. Hardly anyone recognized my university, and many of the other students in the internship were from Harvard or Wharton Business School—Ivy League schools. I felt intimidated so I just tried to do my best and work hard, being the first one in and the last one to leave, and I earned enough credibility to ask questions and learn from the professionals.

By the end of the summer, Merrill Lynch offered me a full-time position to start upon completion of my degree from UBC, which I was quick to accept.

I returned to Canada to finish my degree. My parents were happy that I had earned the opportunity, but they also expressed some sadness and apprehension about my moving across the continent. I was so excited to leave for New York that my father thought I would never come back and work with him, which had been his plan for years.

During my last year in Vancouver, I didn't really have a chance to earn a lot of money. I was living on scholarships and teaching piano. I then moved back to New York full-time and brought all the money I had saved—just $3,000—with me after graduation.

My first day on the job was September 10, 2001. That's when I started on the New York trading floor of Merrill Lynch's options desk.

The next day, everything changed.

Resilience

It was eight thirty on a warm, late-summer morning on my second day on the job at Merrill Lynch's headquarters in lower Manhattan. I was coming out of our morning meeting, eager to get started at my desk amidst five hundred trading stations. I noticed my colleagues staring at the large television screens showing images of a burning tower. I asked what was happening. "Looks like some idiot just flew a Cessna into the World Trade Center (WTC). He must have been drunk." I thought it looked like something out of a movie, even though, in reality, it was much closer to home, as I was standing in the building connected to the WTC by a walkway over the West Side Highway. I heard my manager telling some nearby traders to get back to work as the market opened in less than an hour, and being the new kid, I hurried back to my desk to prepare.

My parents had told me before I moved to New York that if anything ever happened, I was to call home immediately. So, being the dutiful daughter, I did just that. My parents were watching the news, though it was only 5:30 a.m. in Vancouver. I told them what I had heard, not to worry, and that everything was okay, and my dad told me to get back to work. The attention on the screens faded, until about ten minutes later, when wham! The impact was huge, and our building shook. Though we were only on the fifth floor of the building, startled looks around the trading floor triggered some staff to start leaving the building, though there was no real sense of panic. Our managers kept us cool by reminding us that there had been a bomb threat in 1996, which turned out to be just a scare and that the market was to open in less than an hour.

A colleague told me to grab my purse and leave with her. When we got outside, one of my other colleagues became hysterical. I put my hand on her shoulder and asked her, "What's wrong?" Stuttering, she said she had just seen two people leaping from the WTC building next to us, holding hands as they fell through the sky—on fire. I felt a cold shudder throughout my body but couldn't get myself to turn around and look.

Distinct images of frantic and chaotic events flashed everywhere: people cashing out their limits at every ATM, streams of paper flying through the dust-ridden air as the blast force of the collapsing towers thrust papers from the offices above. The hot sun blazing down upon my colleagues and me. Our skin dripped with sweat as we ran up the West Side Highway, away from the burning towers. We were running and feeling lost, totally lost, not knowing where to go. I kept thinking we might run too far and reach Midtown where the famous Empire State building stood, which could very well be the next target. But we couldn't stay where we were; we had to keep moving. Sirens and screams of panic pierced my ears every way I turned. The smell of burning flesh and debris filled my nose.

And that's when it hit me. A wave of fear and overpowering sense of absolute homelessness poured over me like a pail of cold water. I had nowhere to go and no one to help me. I was completely alone. I had just moved to New York City solely for the job. I didn't know anyone. My apartment and everything I owned was just a few blocks from Ground Zero. My cell phone was dead, and there was no reception anyway, because the main cell towers had fallen with the Twin Towers. Never in my life had I felt such a deep blow to my foundational sense of safety. All I kept thinking was I had told my parents after the first plane hit that everything was fine. So I had to make sure that it was.

Later that evening as dusk fell and the dust was settling, I stood, in aching pain, on the corner of Bleecker Street and Third Avenue, resting my blistered feet after running all day in the hot September sun. My new black work dress, nylon stockings, and high heels were covered in a thick layer of dust. I recall staring in bewilderment at the new horizon. Gone were the iconic Twin Towers, and in their place was crumbled, burning rubble.

I came across a colleague who invited me to his apartment to check my messages and call my family. One of the messages was from a distant second cousin, Judy, who lived in New York City and who had located my number from my parents. She left her address and said I could stay with her if I needed a place. I had nothing but the clothes on my back, $30 in cash, and a dead cell phone, so I humbly walked through the streets of lower Manhattan until I found Judy's studio apartment in West Village and knocked on her door. She graciously took me in, and I will forever be grateful.

The next few days were difficult. I was not able to get access to my apartment in Battery Park City because it was considered part of Ground Zero, which meant I still had no access to my passport or any of my belongings should I have wished to leave the city. Aside from Judy's graciousness, I was alone and had nowhere to go. In a moment of despair, I went into her bathroom to take a shower and let the running water mask the sounds of my uncontrolled sobbing. It was then that I realized I had to make a choice: crumble in fear amidst the uncertainty or find a way forward. As my mother had years ago, I faced a challenging fork in the road riddled with risk and clouded by fear. And as my mother had, I found the courage to choose the path that had the greatest chance of leading to a positive outcome, even if it wasn't the easy thing to do. From that point on, I chose to find a way forward. I took what I believed to be a Smart Risk.

Three days later (Friday, September 14), I was back at work, summoned to our emergency off-site trading floor in Jersey City, with my game face on. After going back to Vancouver, briefly, to see my family, I stayed to live and work in New York for another five years. But the impact of that experience shook me to my core and led to fundamental changes in my perspective and actions.

It has taken me many years to realize the impact this experience had on my life and how it has led me to develop a career helping others find resilience in the face of obstacles. Today, more than a decade later, people seek my help in making some of the most important financial and emotional decisions on retirement, selling a business, or even a death or birth. It has taught me how to step away from the emotional fog that can blind us and to know that in times of crisis, there is a way forward if you are willing to look at the situation with a clear and open mind.

It's also shown me that in great times of stress and uncertainty, leadership is extremely important. Those times are often when the greatest opportunities arise, but it takes leadership to seize them. Now, when other people start panicking, I see it as an opportunity to make a difference. The Chinese language has a character for danger and opportunity: *wei chi*. Crisis = danger plus opportunity.

More challenges to come

In the months that followed the 9/11 crisis, the economy took a turn for the worse, and there were a lot of layoffs, which had an even further negative impact on morale. I could have gone back to Vancouver and chosen a safer, perhaps easier way of starting off, but I chose to stay. I knew that my work had not yet been done.

I had worked hard for this opportunity, and I also felt that it was right for me to stay and help where I could. Despite the layoffs and cost cutting, there was huge demand for our services. I worked in equity derivatives and options, which was one area that really benefitted from volatility in the market because when volatility goes up, the demand for options goes up as well.

It was a time of significant growth for my department. There was a real need for people with derivatives expertise, and I got to take on a lot of responsibility in a short period of time. I wasn't afraid to show up first, stay the latest, ask lots of questions, and do the work to add value. Within a year, my manager gave me much more responsibility, and I was covering institutional clients across the United States. They were flying me to San Francisco, Texas—all across the country—to help build the derivatives business for Merrill Lynch.

I learned a lot during that time. And the most important lesson was that when unexpected things happen, it takes resilience and a helping hand to find a way forward.

Jump ahead to five years into my career on Wall Street; I had the job of my dreams. I had accepted an offer from Eton Park Capital, an award-winning hedge fund in Manhattan that had been seeded by Goldman Sachs. They had tailored a role for me, based on my ideal job description. I was invited into the inner circle of their elite investment team that managed over $5 billion for Ivy League university pension funds and New York investors with ultra-high net worth.

It was my job to help analyze and execute on investment ideas that required specialized expertise across equities, options, futures, and convertible bonds. As I worked hard to learn and contribute, I was given increasing responsibility. This additional responsibility included trading the North American markets during the day (getting into the office at six o'clock in the morning), as well as the Asian markets (starting with Japan at seven o'clock in the evening).

The company had built a secure trading station in my Manhattan city apartment so that I could trade the Asian markets every evening past midnight. Then I would go to sleep only to wake up at five o'clock the next morning to start in the Midtown office at six o'clock again. While it was a long work week, from Sunday night with Asia's opening until Friday afternoon when the US market closed, the intellectual stimulation and the pride and prestige of working for one of the most respected investment teams on Wall Street meant that there were many bright and hard-working analysts and traders who wanted my job.

As part of the "inner circle" investment team for this leading New York financial firm, I learned important lessons about how to successfully navigate the challenging investment environment, using modern strategies and tools that helped create exponential money growth for our wealthy investors. In particular, I learned how you don't have to be ultra-wealthy to apply the secrets of successful investing, and this book can be a guide.

Investors today still face great uncertainty

Today, people who are thinking seriously about retirement often express worry because there is so much uncertainty and so much information streaming from the Internet, newsletters, TV, and the media in general that they don't know which direction to take. Investors face many challenges today, and often, they get motivated and then get stuck or procrastinate until it's almost too late.

There is a way to be proactive in building wealth and not losing it. It comes from combining both the art and science of managing wealth through taking Smart Risks.

Taking Smart Risks is a process of decision making that begins with understanding the trade-offs for each choice, considering the probability and magnitude of each outcome, and finally, comparing those to your tolerance for each before making a decision.

Smart Risk Investing involves gathering information, weighing the likelihood and impact of each outcome, comparing those investment outcomes to your tolerance for each, and then taking positive action that increases your chance for successfully reaching your financial purpose and goals. In short, it helps you make reasonable financial decisions that continually stack the odds of success in your favour for long-term financial success.

Oftentimes, people will take the path of least resistance to avoid loss or pain, but in so doing, they continue down a slippery slope taking them farther away from their goals. Taking a Smart Risk approach often starts with thinking differently about risk and then taking a different, more advantageous course of action. If investors don't have the necessary skills or competence, they can work with a team of advisors to make financial success a reality.

In order to achieve that reality, most investors have to challenge their own preconceived notions, prejudices, and assumptions about their finances. Once they open their minds to the challenges in front of them, their team of advisors can help keep them on the right path.

Challenge #1: Investing in volatile markets

One of the key challenges investors face today is the ever-present specter of volatility in global markets. Things can feel good when you are invested in the markets or in real estate and prices are going up. You think you're going to be all set for retirement. And then something terrible and unexpected comes along, and just when you need leadership, there is none because everything is falling and everybody's afraid.

It's how you react in this type of scenario that defines true ability and resilience. One important example of a challenging period of volatility was the global financial crisis of 2007–2008. I left New York in 2006 to partner with my father and grow his Vancouver-based wealth management business. We were advising high-net-worth individuals and families. In 2007 we had grown cautious about the high valuations and speculative fever that had spread from the US housing bubble into the stock market.

We had been advising clients to sell their US stock holdings in early 2008 before the crisis developed, but we were still shocked at the magnitude of the market sell-off as it spread to the rest of the world. When the major brokerage firm, Lehman Brothers, failed in the fall of 2008, it was another huge shock to the system. I had many friends who worked at Lehman in New York. I couldn't believe it was happening.

Instead of hiding under our desks from the bad news raining down on investors everywhere, we took the position of coming in early to call all of our clients to tell them what was happening and advise them not to get too scared with what they were hearing on the news. We wanted them to keep an even, stable view of what was happening and not to overreact. We helped them see the opportunities beyond the fog of immediate uncertainty.

The message we gave was clear: Let's use this opportunity to switch from low-priced assets to low-priced assets with higher quality. Everything's on sale, so let's upgrade the portfolio. Let's invest in the best companies that are paying a dividend. (At that point, the share prices were down so much that the dividend yields were quite high.) Let's upgrade and get you paid to wait until the markets recover.

We recognized the need for leadership at this turbulent time and decided to hold a seminar for the community to which we brought two leading portfolio managers from the East Coast to share that message. We invited our clients to attend, and we opened up the seminar to the community, free of charge. Over 230 people showed up. There was standing room only. We held that seminar on March 3, 2009. The stock market actually bottomed a few days later, so we were conducting the seminar in the depths of despair.

But, by doing so, we helped our clients get through the terrible financial crisis. We showed them how to be opportunistic by transitioning into good dividend-paying companies as well as other nontraditional alternative investments designed to profit in volatile markets. Over the years, the securities rebounded significantly. It worked out handsomely for our clients, and many are in a much stronger financial position today than ever before.

Volatility is always going to be present or lurking around the corner. Having the expertise available to understand and implement strategies using better investment tools will become more and more important. In other words, buffering investment portfolios in times of volatility requires having many more tools available in the investment tool kit today.

Challenge #2: Investors' traditional portfolios may be outdated

One basic tenet of investing is that diversification reduces risk. Diversification refers to holding a sufficient number of investments in a portfolio, with prices that move independently, up or down, based on different factors, so that over time the volatility (a.k.a. price swings) of the individual holdings offset each other, and thus, the overall portfolio volatility is lower than simply owning one investment.

During the period between 1980 and 2007, many investors enjoyed relatively stable returns and average volatility holding a simple and traditional mix of stocks and bonds (often called the traditional 60/40 portfolio, referring to a portfolio holding 60 percent in stocks and 40 percent in bonds).

However, since the great financial crisis of 2008, that all changed. Individual investors experienced historically large losses in 2007–2008 even if they thought they were diversified by holding a 60/40 portfolio. Prices of assets that used to move in opposite directions behaved in a more correlated (similar direction) fashion. For instance, while bond prices increased 2.7 percent during the crisis, that gain did little to offset the 26 percent loss investors experienced in equities in their 60/40 balanced portfolios.

Thus, leading endowment fund managers at Yale University and Harvard University, responsible for managing billions of dollars in pensions, have shifted away from this traditional 60/40 mix to achieve lower risk and better returns for their pension holders. According to a Deutsche Bank study of over four hundred pension and endowment funds, managing over $1.8 trillion in assets, 39 percent of fund managers shifted away from the 60/40 approach in 2014 (up from just 25 percent in 2013) to a more risk-adjusted methodology. Adding alternative investments to a traditional portfolio of stocks and bonds has been shown to lower the volatility, while adding to returns over a full market cycle of approximately seven to ten years.

In many ways, resilience is lacking in investors' traditional portfolios. Canadian portfolios, in particular, tend to be overly concentrated in Canadian stocks and bonds. Even many Canadian mutual funds tend to have almost identical holdings in their top ten stocks. So people who think they're diversified are often not.

Also, many investors have parked money under the mattress out of fear of losing their capital. But what they're doing is stacking the odds against themselves. They are making it more difficult to reach a critical mass of financial assets for achieving financial freedom; they are actually being counterproductive.

Investors today need leadership and strategies that use more refined investment tools to create resilience within their portfolios. Consider investments that are not correlated—meaning their prices don't move in the same direction as stocks and bonds—in order to achieve true diversification. Also, consider the investment paradigm, or point in the economic cycle, in which you are investing. If you don't consider this, you may be in for a shock because what worked well in a secular bull market may suddenly stop working in a sideways or bear market.

> **Secular bull market** – a long-term market trend that lasts five to twenty-five years, consisting of larger positive and smaller negative market trends during this period. Strong investor sentiment drives prices higher, as there are more net buyers than sellers.
>
> **Sideways market** – a market condition where the price trend fluctuates without a clear uptrend or downtrend.
>
> **Bear market** – a market condition in which the prices of securities are falling and widespread pessimism causes the selling to continue.

When our team works with clients, we use an investment process that actively measures and signals which types of assets are favoured from a risk-versus-return perspective to align ourselves with market conditions. We also use active stop losses and targeted profit taking as well as nontraditional (also known as "alternative") investment assets to manage and reduce risk. This allows us to build more truly diversified portfolios, designed to better weather volatile markets. Also, importantly, we use financial planning tools that simplify and bring everything home so the clients understand the real impact these strategies have on their unique circumstances, helping them overcome the uncertainty that otherwise might have held them back from making the smart choice.

Challenge #3: Emotions and money

Another challenge to investors is their humanity. Emotions affect decisions about money. In fact, much of what drives the markets is psychology and subjective analysis. With so much information bombarding investors from unreliable sources, there is the additional challenge of separating the important signals from the distracting noise. For many investors, it's easy to lose sight of reality when an investment has a compelling story that appeals to their emotions. Once the decision has been made, often an argument or rationale is found *afterward* to support the decision. Investors are also tempted to come up with a decision based on something completely unrelated to what is actually going to affect the security's price. Decisions to buy or sell and other business decisions are often made using non-business criteria.

In particular, the emotions of fear and greed affect financial decision making in powerful ways. Greed can tempt people into get-rich-quick and speculative stock tips or lead them to take on more risk than they should. Fear, on the other hand, can lead investors to become too conservative, making investments they perceive to be secure. For instance, investors may think they are safe by parking their cash in term deposits or low-yielding bonds. But this overly safe behaviour may adversely affect them and prevent them from reaching their goals. A good advisor strives to get investors over this hump, which often requires a shift in mind-set.

This book is designed to enable an alternative way of thinking and outlines a process for taking risks to achieve goals, including an active retirement, referred to as the Work-Optional Life.

> Work-Optional Life means having the freedom to live the lifestyle you choose. It means you have the ability to enjoy your preferred lifestyle without having to physically work for it. It means going to work is by choice, not by necessity, since you will have built alternative sources of passive investment income to fund your active lifestyle.

This book outlines a Smart Risk Investing Roadmap as a process that begins with building a foundation of resilience and then encourages growth and achievement through positive action. Think of bamboo. It grows tall and bends with the wind, but underneath, it has deep roots of resilience.

Roots of resilience

Personal resilience and emotional fortitude are two lessons I have learned from overcoming struggles and crises over the years, but I have also benefited from a strong family foundation. Growing up, I regularly heard stories about the great struggles my ancestors' faced as immigrants from China to Canada.

My great-grandfather immigrated to Canada in 1918 to work on building railroads. But he soon realized that when they sent Chinese workers into the mountain tunnels with dynamite, few ever came out. It wasn't really a great career opportunity.

So on his own, my great-grandfather started selling produce door to door. Eventually, he saved up enough money to buy a wheelbarrow. Then he used that wheelbarrow to carry more produce through the neighborhood. He saved enough to eventually buy a grocery store in Burnaby, a suburb of Vancouver. Bit by bit, he saved until he could afford to bring his family from China to Canada, one at a time. Over the years, he and his family worked in the grocery stores, which expanded. He helped build a strong foundation for the multigenerational development of an empire of numerous commercial and residential real estate properties throughout the Lower Mainland of British Columbia, Canada.

I learned a lot from the struggles he faced—struggles that included not being allowed to vote or get a formal education because he was Chinese. I respected the great sacrifices he made for the long-term success of his family, overcoming many disadvantages to be able to create a multigenerational family tree and wealth that has cascaded across the generations. In fact, one of the stipulations he made in the trust he left as a legacy was that, each year, some of the investment proceeds would go toward hosting a large celebration for the entire family (now five generations) to feast and remember their ancestors in a respectful tradition called *bai san*.

My dad is my business partner, and he's also been a major influence in my life. I learned a lot about resilience from my dad. He was born in a rough part of Vancouver just after the Second World War, when times were difficult. He survived by using street smarts and a little bit of grit.

I learned from him that life is about how you deal with adversity—finding a way to overcome your circumstances. There was a lot of racial discrimination against Chinese people in his neighborhood. And on that side of town, you either had to find a way to survive or you didn't.

Hearing his stories throughout my life helped me move forward when I faced times of difficulty. We both attended the University of British Columbia (UBC), where the motto is "Tuum est," which is Latin for "It's up to you."

Redirect your adversary's force

When it comes to combatting risk, I've taken the UBC motto to heart. Developing a broad and deep understanding of the different tools available in your investment toolkit is vital to success in any market. As a young woman, I studied martial arts and found them to be highly valuable, both mentally and physically. In judo, you use the force of your opponent to your advantage. The force of the opponent is against you, but you actually learn to roll with it and turn it into your own momentum. This concept can be applied successfully in investment strategies and is the root of the Smart Risk Investing Roadmap we use today.

Capability is highlighted in times of challenge

My real joy as an advisor to clients comes from being able to help others take action and overcome the key challenges of volatile markets, outdated investment strategies, or emotional obstacles holding them back from building wealth. Even if clients are resistant to taking action initially, my goal as their advisor is to be a catalyst in their lives, to help them surmount the obstacles preventing them from achieving their true goals, which are, most often, to grow a sustainable, active retirement or multigenerational legacy.

Throughout this book I will share the tools and lessons learned from my work with ultra-wealthy investors and show readers how to embrace volatility, consider nontraditional investment strategies to expand the investment tools in their tool kit, and recognize the impact of emotions on money issues so they can overcome challenges to achieving their financial goals.

SUMMARY

- Resilience is a key component in building a sustainable strategy for financial success.
- Investors today face great challenges including volatile global markets, outdated investment tools, and emotional obstacles amidst great informational noise preventing them from making objective decisions.
- The Smart Risk Investing Roadmap is designed to help investors (1) see past the emotional fog of investing to more rationally and objectively assess the likelihood of possible outcomes and (2) compare risk to reward in a prudent and disciplined way to make decisions that consistently stack the odds in their favour, keeping them on the path to long-term financial success.

QUESTIONS

1. How resilient is your current financial situation to pressures that may arise from an unexpected event, like an accident, illness, loss of income, significant rise in interest rates, or a downturn in the housing market or the economy?
2. How would you define personal financial success, today and looking into the future, so you can sleep soundly every night?
3. What challenges have you faced, so far, in pursuing financial success?
4. What is holding you back, right now, from overcoming these challenges?
5. What are the crises or challenges facing you right now that could turn out to be opportunities?

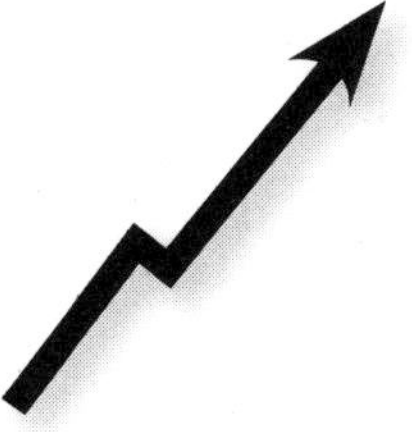

CHAPTER 2

The Biggest Mistakes Investors Make

We cannot solve our problems with the same thinking we used to create them.
—Albert Einstein

We all have biases when we make investment decisions, and often we don't even know it. I have seen it with many clients, from the most successful, multibillion-dollar institutional clients in New York City, to my retired clients living off the income from their investments. Emotions and psychological biases have an impact on how we all make financial decisions. In this chapter, we will explore the mental barriers, mistakes, and obstacles people face when dealing with money, to help you overcome these impediments to wealth building.

Many of the biggest mistakes are rooted in the way people think and feel about money. The science of money is that money is a store of value that can be exchanged for goods and services. Often, it's the art, or emotional, part of the money equation that drives our monetary decisions.

How we see money, along with our beliefs concerning money, reflect deep biases. Part of the value a financial advisor provides to clients is the ability to recognize these biases and help clients understand them before applying thoughtful solutions to move one step forward at a time.

Information is a positive; an overload of information is not. There is almost too much information available today, and people can become paralyzed by it. They often freeze and follow the path of least resistance or do nothing. Too much information can lead us to make decisions using our intuition rather than facts and evidence.

Introducing Victor and Nancy

Let me share a story about a couple named Victor and Nancy. I was first introduced to Victor, a sixty-year-old physician, in 2007. Victor was married to Nancy, a teacher, and together they had three adult sons. Over the years, Victor and Nancy established about $3 million in stocks, bonds, mutual funds, and real estate investments. But these investments were held in multiple accounts at three different brokerage houses. Victor expressed particular concern over one portfolio that consisted of risky junior oil and gas and gold companies that was losing money—even in a strong market.

He was introduced to me by an existing client who had asked if I would meet him and help him make better progress with his investments. As a service to my clients, I make myself available to their friends and family, and so Victor called to make an appointment to meet. When we met, he explained that he was tired of his investments not working for him. He was so busy running his medical practice that he paid little attention to his investment portfolio. He wanted to work less, spend more time travelling with Nancy, and ultimately, enjoy freedom from his day job of attending to patients and being on call at the hospital.

Victor was feeling stagnant, tired, and frustrated. He wanted his investments to be working for him, providing a regular cash flow similar to what we had structured for his friend. I asked Victor to describe in detail how he had been investing for the past ten years. He had been repeating several common investment mistakes that were holding him and his family's financial situation back from its true potential.

1. Be intellectual, not intuitive.
2. Be proactive, not reactive.
3. Act by design, not by default.
4. Embrace change; don't resist change.

Among the mistakes I see investors make is acting from an *intuitive perspective*. We help clients shift toward more of an *intellectual framework*. The second big mistake is being *reactive*. Our goal is to get clients to be *proactive*. Third, investors can improve their financial situation by acting not by default but *by design***.** And fourth, they often feel stuck or *resist change*. The goal is to move them toward being able to make these changes and to empower them to control their own financial future.

Be intellectual, not intuitive

Sometimes your instincts and gut feelings are the result of your real-life experiences. But a robust investment strategy with solid, repeatable results requires that you think carefully about your next move, not rely on your emotions. Human intuition can fool us in predictable and consistent ways. The growing scientific field of behavioural finance has shown that we assume we are in control of our decisions when, in reality, we're not.

Consider a systematic, reasoned investment process to strip away the emotion, weed out human biases, and allow us to make sound financial decisions. This idea serves as the basis of the Smart Risk Investing framework, using an intellectually disciplined process for investing, instead of one based on emotion. So to avoid these pitfalls of cognitive illusions, beware of the newsletters and investment professionals toting expertise based on intuition and predictions about the future.

Psychologist Daniel Kahneman has done a lot of work in this field. His book *Thinking, Fast and Slow* highlights several decades of research across a variety of fields showing that people place too much confidence in subjective, human judgment—whether it's predicting earthquakes, sports betting, changes in the weather, investment, and so on.

Human predictions and intuitions face many limitations. One example is *loss avoidance*. Everyone hates to lose, so much that we tend to feel the pain of losing $50 twice as much as the joy of winning $100. In Victor's case, he had been holding on to a pile of losing investments to avoid the pain of realizing a loss. But on the flip side, Victor explained, he had a tendency to sell his winning investments too soon. He simply didn't want to lose.

Statistically, it's been shown that investors are better off holding on to or adding to their winners and cutting their losing positions short. But it's hard to actually do that. So we build *stop losses* into our investment process where appropriate. Stop losses are trigger points at certain pre-defined thresholds where the securities are sold to limit further losses. Kahneman's research shows that investors have exaggerated bias against losses and a hindsight bias that gives them the false sense that the future is predictable.

The other mistake that comes across a lot is *anchoring*. People give excessive importance to the price that they paid for an investment and refuse to take action until it returns to their original investment level. But in reality, the opportunity cost of that money may be better placed in another investment, regardless of what the investor paid for it.

Another pitfall is *overconfidence bias*. We all tend to attribute good results to our own decisions, but we blame bad results on someone else. Once we have made a decision, we unconsciously seek out information patterns to support that decision. This is called *confirmation bias*. Another hazard is *herding*. People take comfort in doing something that everyone else is doing. Victor shared with me that he had once bought a large amount of a speculative gold stock because his friend was buying it. But this bias doesn't just happen among individuals. It happens among institutions, hedge funds, and smart, educated, and wealthy people, like those who invested with the fraudster Bernie Madoff. He was regarded as an elite investment manager, so everyone wanted to be part of that club.

One final important bias I often observe in relation to *intuitive versus intellectual* is the idea that people prefer stories to analysis. We all love a good story, so investors are often enticed to make an investment based on being sold a good story as to why the company's product or service will be the next big thing. Anecdotal personal experience of the company's product or service often leads people to think it will be a good investment. In Victor's case, he had accumulated multiple brokerage accounts over the years before he met us because he had been enticed by stories—stories about a star portfolio manager, or a company producing new technology that was about to become widely adopted, or a new drug that was about to receive regulatory approval.

The data-driven analysis of a company's business fundamentals—the company's ability to earn and sustain cash flow and profit in a real business with predictable results—is often overlooked because it's not as sexy or interesting as that anecdotal story.

Be proactive, not reactive

Building a financial plan can be a great solution for preventing reactive behaviour. However, it's not enough. In addition to a financial plan, investors need a sound, dynamic investment plan designed to take advantage of the changing investment environment and a clear roadmap that proactively anticipates the winding path toward their goals. The risks are great for investors who are not focused and who assume a reactive approach, allowing outside events to influence their choices. It's easy to blame external factors and then defer the pain of ownership, rather than take responsibility for bad choices.

The volatile year of 2008 is an example. Many investors let emotions override rational decisions. Naturally, investors were looking for relief from the pain and anxiety of volatility and falling asset prices. So even if investors had a financial plan, many let their emotions get the best of them, resulting in actions like selling their quality holdings, which provided near-term relief from anxiety but had long-term, devastating results. This is an example of a reactive approach to investment. And at times like these, a rational, proactive approach is hugely rewarding. I'll give you an example. Paul Tudor Jones, the famous multibillionaire and successful investor, made billions of dollars during market crashes because he had the mental fortitude to step in and buy when others were fearful, ultimately making huge profits.

Act by design, not by default

There is also the problem of a stale portfolio that investors maintain because they're afraid of leaving their comfort zone. They may be stuck in a stagnating relationship because they are afraid to leave their advisor or are reluctant to seek professional advice because they have always operated without one. Either way, acting by default can mean accepting mediocrity at the expense of building wealth. It may seem like work to find an advisor when you are used to being in control of all the decisions yourself, but working collaboratively with someone who will put you and your changing needs first is worth the effort. It's not always easy to break from old patterns of behaviour, but remaining stuck in a state of inertia can mean that you get left behind in a world that is constantly evolving.

Embrace change; don't resist change

And that brings me to my last point in this chapter: overcoming resistance to change in order to create empowerment. Change is never easy, and it's human nature to resist change. When it comes to investments, recognizing when it makes sense to change a strategy is important. Yes, investors need to plan, but they also need to be able to adjust their strategy when it makes sense. Humans often get stuck in a state of inertia, preferring to do nothing rather than doing something and risking painful repercussions. It's just the way we're wired. I see it among friends. I see it in clients. I see it in myself at times. But how you deal with it is what matters.

When Victor first came to see me in 2007, he was resistant to change. He had tried investing but kept falling into the same behavioural traps. I explained to him that the first step is to know your limitations and then to know how to adapt so you can succeed. If you don't, you're going to get hurt. I clarified the importance of designing his investment decision-making process to overcome human weaknesses and offset his resistance to change. At that time, he was not yet ready to make the change. He was still allowing himself to invest reactively and was stuck in his resistance to change. In fact, I didn't hear from Victor for another two years.

Overcoming the biggest mistakes

Because Victor was so resistant to change, it took him another two years after our first meeting in 2007 before he finally made the switch to hire us as his advisory team. His catalyst was when the 2007–2008 global financial crisis hit and all three of Victor and Nancy's investment accounts held at various brokerage houses collapsed. Unfortunately, the daily stress and agony of seeing his account values drop caused him enough grief, distraction from his work, and strain on his relationship with Nancy that Victor felt compelled to take action to stop the bleeding. Succumbing to the pain and fear of further losses, Victor followed his intuition to sell everything at deep losses.

My client, and Victor's good friend, had invited him to attend our client seminar in March 2009. The very next day, both Victor and his wife, Nancy, came to meet with me and transfer all of their accounts. We got started right away to put them on the right track.

I was pleased that Nancy joined us at the meeting because I try to encourage spouses or partners to be part of the conversations around their finances. This fosters healthy communication and helps create alignment on important financial goals and expectations. As we sat down together, I asked them how they envisioned their lives in five, ten, and twenty years from that point. Their answers were entirely different, as they had never discussed this together before. He pictured himself still working well into his eighties, though he craved more flexibility and freedom. She wanted him to stop working immediately so they could travel and spend more time with their grandchildren.

We focused on creating plans for Victor and Nancy that followed a Smart Risk Investing framework. First, we developed a financial plan to instill long-term thinking versus short-term reactionary behaviour. This financial plan outlined how much they would need to accomplish their mutual and individual financial goals. Second, we constructed an investment plan designed to capitalize on the current investment landscape based on objective measures of decision making. For this plan, we introduced discretionary management by a professional investment team. Discretionary management gives the advisor and investment professionals the authority to make day-to-day decisions on a client's behalf, operating in alignment with the client's risk tolerance and return objectives. It removes the weight of emotion-based decision making from the shoulders of investors.

Lastly, we built Victor and Nancy a customized roadmap that outlined the way forward over the next several years, tying it all together for them. This roadmap outlined the topics we would discuss during each regularly scheduled review meeting to make sure the plans were still relevant or to make adjustments.

Within a few months of starting our working relationship, Victor and Nancy had their plans in place and had overcome the mistakes that had once held them back. Victor and Nancy realized they weren't equipped to make the decisions in the first place, so deciding to let us take on the responsibility with our professional process and expertise empowered them to move forward in a positive direction, and that's the whole goal.

SUMMARY

- Many of the biggest mistakes investors make are rooted in the way they think and feel about money, making them vulnerable to emotional decision making and predictable patterns of behavioural biases.

- Consider the following four ideas on overcoming the biggest mistakes:

    1. Be intellectual, not intuitive.
    2. Be proactive, not reactive.
    3. Act by design, not by default.
    4. Embrace change; don't resist change.

- Old opinions die hard. Even when the facts and situation change, many investors resist adapting to them. Once they recognize this limitation, they are then in a better position to focus on applying a disciplined process that combines both the science and art of investing, provides clarity amidst the uncertainty, and objectively evolves over time to adapt to changing market conditions.

QUESTIONS

1. How have emotions like fear, greed, gut feelings, affection, anxiety, desire, despair, envy, hope, regret, and overconfidence affected your financial decisions in the past?
2. How did you react to past financial situations that included a large loss? A large gain? What did you learn about yourself in the process?
3. What beliefs do you hold about money, regarding how it should be earned, accounted for, handled, spent, and given away?
4. What experiences did you have with money, while growing up, that affect your beliefs about money today?
5. What is your greatest current concern about money, and how have you chosen to address it (or not)?

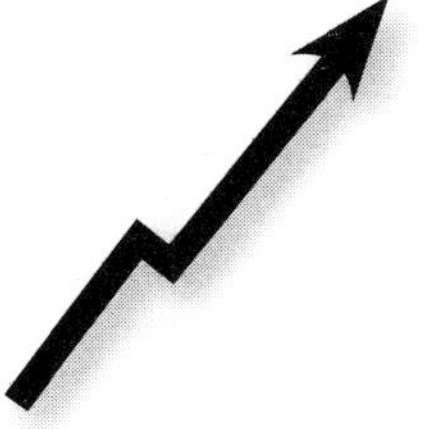

CHAPTER 3

Debunking Common Myths about Money and Investing

Beliefs are hypotheses to be tested, not treasures to be guarded.
— Philip E. Tetlock and Dan Gardner,
authors, *Superforecasting: The Art and Science of Prediction*

Even in today's information-drenched age, myths about investing persist. As we saw in the previous chapter, investors' internal state of mind and belief systems form the foundation of what become their actions. Recognizing some of the common myths about money and investing and their respective antidotes is a key step toward investing as the wealthy do.

Myth #1: Diversification alone is enough to eliminate risk.

When I first met Victor and Nancy back in 2007, they believed they were well diversified and insulated from market downturns by having multiple brokerage accounts holding term deposits and mutual funds. They had about $3 million in total investments split across three different institutions. They believed that they were diversified and less at risk to market downturns because they were dealing with three different brokerage firms and multiple funds. They were shocked to find that during the 2007–2008 crisis all of their investment funds dropped by about the same amount, bearing losses of more than 30 percent over the course of the year, despite being "diversified." None of their term deposits—no matter the issuer—were cashable for another three to five years, so they didn't have the liquidity they needed to even take advantage of the downturn should they have wanted to.

To make matters worse, when they looked closer at their holdings, Victor and Nancy realized each of their mutual funds held approximately eight of the same top ten holdings, giving them a false sense of diversification. They had fallen victim to the myth that diversification alone is enough to reduce risk. The reality is that there can be too much diversification and not enough focus.

To maximize the benefits of diversification, we helped Victor and Nancy put in place a carefully constructed portfolio that included alternative assets with prices that moved in different directions, so the next time the market turned down, Victor and Nancy's alternative assets might appreciate in value to offset any losses in the traditional assets.

There is another problem with diversification. Some investors think that they should diversify their advisors and have two or three or more financial advisors to reduce the risk in dealing with one advisor. However, (1) overdiversifying the number of financial advisors can mean you lose accountability because no single advisor feels responsible for your entire financial well-being, and (2) dealing with multiple advisors can be like having multiple family physicians and revealing only one symptom to each doctor. You tell one of your dizziness, you tell another of your shortness of breath, and you tell another of your family history of heart disease. How do you expect to get a proper diagnosis if each doctor only sees part of the picture? It's similar to collecting loyalty points from three different credit cards. You never really collect enough from each one to buy anything good.

In reality, working with one really good financial advisor who understands your entire financial picture can provide you with a much better comprehensive plan for your financial health. Also, if you're dealing with multiple advisors, you're likely paying multiple account fees. You may be missing out on the VIP treatment you would get if you were with one advisor. If there are too many cooks in the kitchen, the advisors you are dealing with will be unable to do their best work.

One of my clients had worked with as many as six advisors simultaneously over a twenty-year period and then slowly whittled them down to two—and now just me. He's learned that *quality trumps quantity* when working with the right people, and when you find them, you hold them close. Clarity of vision—a view from the outside—is a valuable service we give our clients. Experience is a great teacher, but learning from someone who has been there and can keep you out of harm's way is a better and less painful approach.

Myth #2:
Volatility should be feared.

When I first met Victor, he admitted that the market's ups and downs gave him some angst. While he tried not to obsess over the changes in his monthly statement values, he did profess to get more anxious even though he knew that over the long run he was still ahead. He often worried that a market downturn would erase all of his hard-earned savings.

Dancing with volatility

Investors should not be afraid of volatility. Think of it as dancing with volatility and being mentally prepared for it so that when it does arrive, you can adapt to its direction as you would with an experienced dance partner. Take it a step further: *expect* volatility to happen. Volatility may present risk in the short term but actually creates opportunities for investors with long-term time horizons to get into the market at attractive levels.

Using options to harness volatility

As with judo, take the force of your opponent coming at you and roll with it and turn it around to your advantage. In some cases, using a nontraditional investment approach like an options strategy can help you both reduce risk and increase your profits in a volatile market. While options strategies are often considered to be "high risk," in reality, when used in a smart way, they are quite the opposite. Let me explain.

Let's say you've been considering downsizing your home. You're not in any hurry to sell, but it just so happens that your neighbor approaches you and gives you a good offer. You estimate that you could sell your house on the market for $3 million today. He likes your house, but he's a little worried that the lofty home prices might drop, so he proposes the following:

- He will pay you $50,000 cash today for the right to buy your house for $3.1 million anytime within the next six months.

- He has no obligation to buy it and may walk away from the purchase anytime. His option to buy your house expires in six months.

You think about it and accept his offer. Congratulations, you've just sold him an option. Why did you do this? There are three possible outcomes for you, all of which have their merits:

1. The value of your house rises over the next six months, and your neighbor exercises his option to buy your house for $3.1 million. You have made out quite well, earning $3.1 million *plus* the $50,000 cash payment he paid up front for the option. So you are better off by $150,000 ($3.15 million - $3 million) than if you had sold it on Day 1.

2. The value of your house drops over the next six months. Your neighbor will most likely walk away from the deal, and you still own the house. You keep the $50,000 cash payment he paid you for the option. So while you may have some regrets not selling it on Day 1, you have cushioned your loss with the $50,000 cash premium you received up front and can even repeat this strategy for the next six months to earn some extra cash flow.

3. The third and final possible outcome is that the value of your home remains the same. Your neighbor probably does not buy your house for $3.1 million and walks away from the deal, but you are happy because you have earned yourself a cool $50,000 cash in a flat market, and you still own your house.

What was outlined above is also known as a covered call option strategy. Investors can do the same thing with their stock positions. In volatile markets, the premium (i.e., the $50,000 the neighbor paid for the right to buy the house) tends to be higher, and so the option seller (i.e., you) can earn a nice income just by selling options on stocks already owned. I like to think of it as getting paid a premium (i.e., the $50,000) to put in a specified-price order to sell a stock (or house).

As one of the wealthiest investors I have worked with once said to me, "Everything in life involves risk." Even not doing anything is actually taking a risk. Re-examine the situation to see how the risk or volatility can be turned into your opportunity.

Myth #3: Bonds are safe, and stocks are too risky.

Both bonds and stocks play an important role in building a diversified investment portfolio. But many investors hold too narrow a view of the respective risks, thinking they are safer in bonds than they really are, and conversely, avoiding stocks because they think they are too risky.

Bonds are investments that have a fixed maturity date when investors are guaranteed by the borrower to get all of their initial investment back. Until that maturity date arrives, investors are also promised regular predetermined interest payments as compensation for letting the borrower use their money. Generally, investors consider bonds to be "low-risk" investments because of the guaranteed principal and interest payments. And over the past several years, as interest rates have declined, investors who locked in to receive higher interest payments have been rewarded handsomely as the falling interest rate environment has favoured the market values of those bonds. However, when interest rates head higher, the opposite effect will take place and may affect bond prices in a negative way if investors want to sell the bond before its final maturity date.

Four common risks for bond investors

1. *Interest rate risk.* When interest rates rise, bond prices fall. When interest rates fall, bond prices rise. This is a risk if you need to sell a bond before its maturity date and interest rates are up. You may end up selling the bond for less than you paid for it.

2. *Inflation risk.* This is the risk that the return you earn on your investment doesn't keep pace with inflation. If you hold a bond paying 2 percent interest and inflation becomes 3 percent, your return is actually negative (-1 percent), when adjusted for inflation. You'll still get your principal back when your bond matures, but it will be worth less in terms of dollars adjusted for inflation. Inflation risk increases the longer you hold a bond.

3. *Market risk.* This is the risk that investors will not want to pay as much for your bond as you originally paid for it. If this happens, or if the entire bond market drops, the price of your bond investments will likely fall regardless of the quality or type of bonds you hold. If you need to sell a bond before its maturity date, you may end up selling it for less than you paid for it.

4. *Credit risk.* If you buy bonds from a company or government that ends up in financial trouble, there's a greater risk you'll lose money. This is called credit risk or default risk. Sometimes, the issuer can't make the interest payments to investors. It's also possible the issuer won't pay back the face value of the bond when it matures.

The merits of stocks

Stocks (or equities) also play an important part in an investment portfolio. In particular, consider stocks of companies that consistently deliver a dividend that grows each year. They tend to outperform companies that do not provide a dividend. A "dividend-paying company" is a company whose shares pay a regular dividend (typically a quarterly cash payment) to investors. A "dividend-growing company" is a simply a company whose shares have paid an *increasing* amount in dividends to investors each year. During the period from 1986 to 2014, dividend-growing companies returned an approximate 12.1 percent total return per year, compared to dividend-paying companies that earned investors 10.2 percent. Compare those attractive returns to the TSX (Toronto Stock Exchange) Composite that returned 6.6 percent to investors and to companies that cut dividends that only returned 1.9 percent. Non-dividend-paying companies returned the least, at just 1 percent annualized returns over the same time period.

That's a huge return differential. While they, historically, have generated the highest return, dividend growers also tend to be less risky from a volatility perspective. Comparing standard deviation as a measure of volatility over that same period of time, the dividend growing and paying companies had about a 13 percent annualized volatility, versus the Canadian S&P/TSX Index with about 16 percent volatility and the non-dividend payers with 23 percent volatility. The companies that cut their dividends had the highest volatility at 24 percent.

Hence, a focus on strong dividend-growing companies in your investment process can be worthwhile because both returns and risk are often favourable, and the cash flow from the dividends can be an important source of retirement income and because of the current economic and interest rate environment. The good news is that dividend-growing companies actually tend to do quite well in a rising rate environment that is not highly inflationary.

Changing risk parameters for bonds vs. stocks

While many brokerage houses are required by regulators to have investors sign off on accepting higher risk in order to invest in stocks versus bonds, some brokerage houses that are looking ahead to a rising interest rate environment are now requiring *bond investors* to acknowledge they are willing to accept a higher level of risk associated with bonds. This reflects a changing economic environment to which investors should pay close attention.

Myth #4:
Buy term life insurance and invest the difference.

Term life insurance provides coverage for a tax-free death benefit payment at a fixed rate of payments for a limited period of time.

Permanent life insurance (which may include whole life or universal life insurance) combines a death benefit with a savings or investment account. While the upfront deposits are typically higher than term insurance premiums, permanent plans have a dual tax advantage and hence are popular with the wealthy: the death benefit's tax-free, and earnings in the investment-account part of the plan can accrue tax-free each year.

Term insurance is popular mainly because it's often the cheapest form of insurance, and it's an effective protection tool for those who simply cannot afford more. However, the old adage "Buy term and invest the difference" has many pitfalls, and the wealthiest 1 percent are voting with their dollars. In fact, according to a US Federal Reserve study, 22 percent of assets accumulated tax-free in permanent life policies were held by the wealthiest 1 percent of US families in 2007—those with more than $8.4 million in net worth. More broadly, 55 percent of the assets in such policies were held by the wealthiest 10 percent of families. The bottom half, by net worth, held just 6.5 percent of these assets. The tax savings and benefits of using permanent life insurance for people in high tax brackets, for business owners and for people who wish to preserve their wealth across generations, are staggering.

Other benefits of using permanent life insurance as a tax-advantaged financial planning tool include:

- *True diversification.* The assets in a whole life plan grow at a positive rate each year, and once vested, can never be retracted. This is helpful, particularly when other assets are in decline and offers truly noncorrelated returns—a good thing!

- *Liquidity.* Unlike term insurance, permanent insurance typically has a cash value that can be borrowed against to provide access to capital while you are alive. The liquidity benefits at death are also plentiful, providing much-needed cash at a time when, typically, estate or capital gains taxes are owed.

- *Flexibility.* Unlike term insurance, for which payment schedules are rigid (otherwise, the protection can be lost), permanent life insurance offers a lot more flexibility in terms of changing or deviating from scheduled payments.

Myth #5: I don't need an advisor; the fees are too high.

There is a lot of misunderstanding about fees for financial advisory services. Investors will sometimes compare apples to oranges and focus on the wrong thing. For example, a good advisor can help investors avoid losing large amounts of money, when investors might otherwise succumb to their own emotions and biases and make sub-optimal or short-term decisions. Fees should only become an issue if you're not getting enough value out of the relationship.

What to look for in finding the right advisor for you

- *Experience.* Both the number of years and quality of that experience are key factors to evaluate when hiring the right advisor. In today's world, it's increasingly important to find someone who thinks globally—and therefore can understand a broad set of investment tools—but who also understands the local regulatory and tax constraints clients face. Look for someone who works with clients who have similar goals or face similar constraints as yours, which will put that advisor's experience to your advantage.
- *Smart Risk mind-set.* As important as the level of experience is the quality of an advisor's mind-set and ability to provide value-added service to the relationship.

Look for evidence of a mind-set that actively seeks to gather information, minimizes biases, and routinely tests and makes adjustments to adapt in order to—most importantly—act in the best interests of clients.

- *Trust, accountability, and credibility.* Trust, accountability, and credibility are also key characteristics to look for in an advisor. These characteristics can be verified in many ways. Client endorsements or third-party testimonials can be useful to gain insight into the quality of work the advisor does. Also, an advisor's titles and credentials may reflect the level of education he or she has and the breadth of professional services that he or she is licensed to advise on. In the increasingly complex world of wealth management, which is a knowledge-based industry, more relevant credentials (some listed below) are a positive reflection of an advisor's breadth of knowledge and commitment to continual learning and improvement. An advisor's job is to keep getting smarter in order to help clients navigate the increasingly complex financial world.

Quick guide to investment advisors' accreditation

Acronym	Full Name	Summary
	EMPHASIS ON FINANCIAL PLANNING	
CFP	Certified Financial Planner	Becoming the gold standard for financial planning
PFP	Personal Financial Planner	Focused on banking and financial planning
RFP	Registered Financial Planner	Less common but well established for retirement planning
CLU	Chartered Life Underwriter	Insurance-focused financial advice for estate planning
FEA	Family Enterprise Advisor	Proficiency in multigenerational business family solutions
	EMPHASIS ON MANAGING INVESTMENTS	
CFA	Chartered Financial Analyst	Globally recognized for professional portfolio management, financial planning, and ethics
CIM	Chartered Investment Manager	Focused on portfolio management in Canada
CMT	Chartered Market Technician	Proficiency in technical analysis of the financial markets.

When hiring an advisor, make sure that your service-level expectations are clear to determine if there is a potentially good fit between what you are looking for and what the advisor can and is willing to deliver. People with more basic needs may be well served by someone who has a lower level of licensing and lower fees. People with a higher net worth and investors who aspire to invest as the wealthy do should seek out financial specialists with the highest skill sets and expertise, as they may add the most value to the advisor-client relationship.

It's also important to understand how the fee is charged. In a traditional brokerage account, the fee is charged on a per-transaction basis (i.e., on each buy or sell of a security). For mutual funds, often an upfront fee is charged, and there is also an ongoing annual management fee that covers the cost of professional management. In a fee-based brokerage account, a flat annual fee is charged for professional advisory services instead of a commission charged on each transaction. Many investors feel that this type of fee-based account generally aligns advisors with their clients' interests. In a fee-based brokerage account, the advisor works to find the best solution designed to grow the portfolio over time and satisfy the client in the long term. Often, in nonregistered accounts, this fee is also considered tax-deductible. In Canada, only about 20 percent of advisors offer strictly fee-based services, while in the USA it's more than 60 percent and rising.

In a fee-based brokerage account, clients often pay a management fee to the advisor for advice and may also pay additional fees for the management of the investment product the advisor is suggesting (i.e., fees paid to the third party managing the funds). However, some advisors have the requisite investment management skills—those with a CFA or CIM designation can be licensed as portfolio managers—to perform many of the same functions as a mutual fund manager and can perform these functions directly, thus saving the client a layer of third-party management fees.

Matching the client with the right advisor

Finding the right advisor is a little bit like a courtship. In addition to the expertise and credibility fit, you may look beyond the initial chemistry to get a deeper understanding of your advisor candidates. What drives them? What are their core philosophies on money, wealth management, and investing? What is their investment process, and how do they execute? What are their commitments to clients? It's not so much about proximity as it is about their having the right attitude to helping you meet your goals and the technical skills to be able to do so, as well as their commitment to continual improvement.

Do you meet the advisor's criteria?

Remember, with the increasing complexity in today's financial world, good advisors are in high demand. So you may want to consider the criteria a leading advisor will be looking for when deciding whether to accept a new client. Before accepting a new client, many sought-after advisors will consider not only the prospective client's asset size and trajectory as criteria but also the prospect's attitude and potential to become an advocate.

SUMMARY

Recognizing and debunking some of the common myths about money and their respective antidotes is a key step toward investing as the ultra-wealthy do. Below is a summary of six key myths and their antidotes:

- Myth #1: Diversification alone is enough to eliminate risk.
    - Reality: Over diversification can limit success. Consider strategies that take into account which risks you wish to reduce, and then build a strategy that isolates those risks while allowing you to address risk in a smarter way. Focus on having the right advisors in your circle of trust; focus on quality, not quantity.
- Myth #2: Volatility should be feared.
    - Reality: Volatility creates opportunity. Option strategies can help you profit from volatile markets.
- Myth #3: Bonds are safe, and stocks are too risky.
    - Reality: Depending on the market environment, bonds may be as volatile as stocks.
- Myth #4: Buy term insurance and invest the difference.
    - Reality: People are often better off purchasing permanent life insurance rather than term insurance in the long run, particularly wealthy investors.

☼ Myth #5: I don't need an advisor; the fees are too high.

- Reality: Surrounding yourself with smart, experienced, credible people who have your best interests at heart can be invaluable. Be open-minded to diversity of thought, elevating you to new levels of success.

QUESTIONS

1. Which of these myths are you holding on to regarding your own money?
2. Which of these myths are holding you back from the financial outcomes you want and need?
3. What changes would be required of you to let go of these restricting myths?
4. Which myths are you ready to let go of right now if it means better financial results for you and your family?
5. How would it feel if you could move beyond these myths and were able to reach your financial goals sooner?

PART TWO

The Smart Risk Investing Roadmap to Achieving Financial Freedom

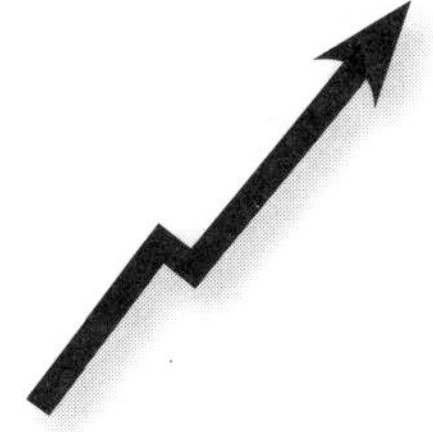

CHAPTER 4

Introducing the Smart Risk Investing Roadmap and the Five Ps

"Distinguishing the signal from the noise requires both scientific knowledge and self-knowledge."
—Nate Silver, author, *The Signal and the Noise: Why Most Predictions Fail – but Some Don't*

Being busy does not always mean real work. The object of all work is production or accomplishment and to either of those ends there must be forethought, system, planning, intelligence, and honest purpose, as well as perspiration. Seeming to do is not doing.
—Thomas Edison

It can be a long and winding road between where investors are and where they want to be financially. Investors face many obstacles along the way, like volatile markets, higher costs of living, emotional decision making, and sudden life events. Often, the main things holding people back from making significant financial progress are not someone else's limitations but rather their own limiting perceptions, beliefs, and expectations. Consider a framework that involves taking Smart Risks to overcome these obstacles to achieving your financial goals.

The Smart Risk Investing Roadmap is designed to help investors see past the emotional fog of investing to rationally and objectively assess probabilities of outcomes and compare risk versus reward in a prudent and disciplined way, allowing them to make choices that consistently stack the odds in their favour and keeping them on the path to long-term financial success.

Consider a roadmap on which the guideposts help you move past obstacles to long-term financial success. Financial success may include achieving and maintaining a Work-Optional Life, followed by a successful period beyond active retirement, and finally, creating your lasting legacy. Let's begin by understanding these guideposts I call the Five Ps: purpose, people, plan, perspective, and positive action.

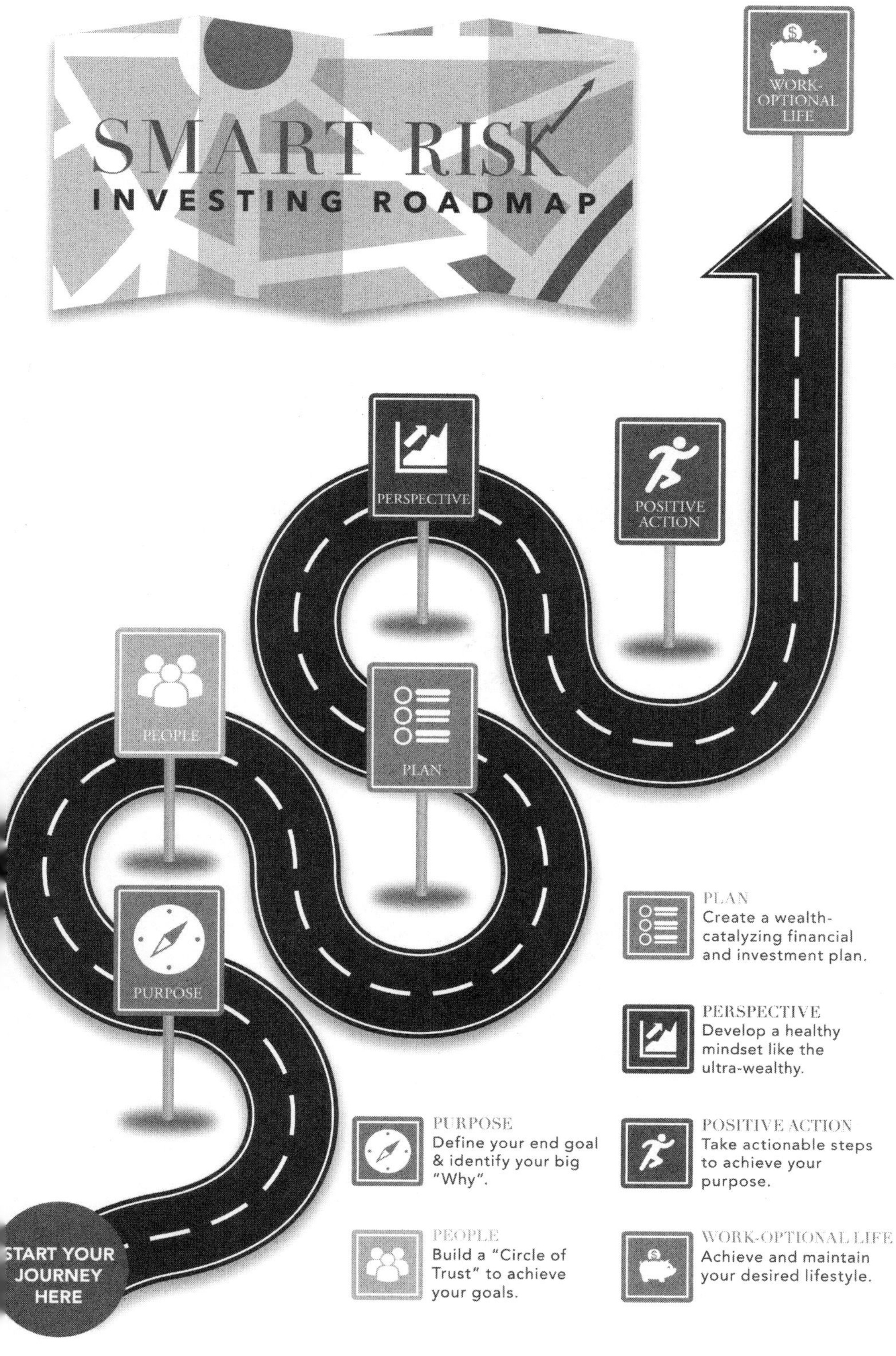

SMART RISK INVESTING ROADMAP

WORK-OPTIONAL LIFE

PERSPECTIVE

POSITIVE ACTION

PEOPLE

PLAN

PURPOSE

START YOUR JOURNEY HERE

PLAN
Create a wealth-catalyzing financial and investment plan.

PERSPECTIVE
Develop a healthy mindset like the ultra-wealthy.

PURPOSE
Define your end goal & identify your big "Why".

POSITIVE ACTION
Take actionable steps to achieve your purpose.

PEOPLE
Build a "Circle of Trust" to achieve your goals.

WORK-OPTIONAL LIFE
Achieve and maintain your desired lifestyle.

The Five Ps: Guideposts for getting past obstacles to investing:

Purpose

The first guidepost is purpose. Begin with your end goals in mind to understand what really motivates you around money decisions, your *why*. Your end goals may include having enough saved up in retirement so you have the freedom and flexibility to never work again. They may include being able to support a university education for each of your grandchildren or perhaps leaving a legacy to a charity that helps a global cause you wish to support. There may be a few or many financial goals that give great purpose for your money. Once you have a list, rank these goals from highest to least important, and we will explore the concept of purpose in more depth in the next chapter.

People

The second guidepost is people. The quality of people around you really matters. Consider building your own personal board of directors. By this, I mean surround yourself with a trustworthy and highly competent team of people who may include family members, a few close friends, and your professional advisors, particularly those with wealth and estate-planning expertise, tax expertise, financial expertise, and medical expertise, and possibly, others with whom you can develop a lasting relationship. It's important for this advisory board to be experienced, resourceful, and have your best interests at heart.

Consider including those who don't simply agree with everything you say, because diversity of thought encourages a constant state of evolution. While individual perspectives and lenses of experience may vary, everyone needs to be working toward a common purpose: your overall success in achieving your goals. In rugby, athletes call this type of team approach a *scrum*. On the Tour de France, bikers form small teams called *pelotons* to reduce drag and therefore accelerate their advantage and speed to the finish line. Some executive management teams call such a group a *wolf pack* or *mastermind group*. For my clients, I call it a *circle of trust*.

Building a circle of trust will open your mind-set to new and productive ideas. But it's not enough just to have these people around you. Introduce them to each other so they can operate and communicate as a cohesive team when necessary. When you fall, they are there to pick you up. Failure is a necessary part of making progress, and your circle of trust is there to help you grow from the experience and become stronger.

When is a good time to create one? Consider having these advocates in place in the initial stage of your path to financial success. This is why I place this guidepost early in the Smart Risk Investing Roadmap. Working with these advocates early is important to ensure the roadmap is in place well before old age, as the risk of cognitive decline increases. We will discuss these plans further in chapter 6.

It's not always easy to find advisors who are willing to ask powerful questions that clients may not be able to easily answer. It takes courage, empathy, and a genuine care for the client if advisors are to be catalysts in their client's journey, propelling them over a hump of inertia toward financial freedom and helping them find a deep-rooted, authentic sense of safety and security. Once you have established a team of highly competent people whom you can trust to have your best interests at heart, hold them close, as they will prove to be invaluable to your long-term success.

Let me share a story about a long-time client, Dr. Ellen. Dr. Ellen had been practicing as a family doctor for over thirty years, and her patients absolutely adored her. But there came a time as she approached her sixty-sixth birthday that she felt ready to begin the next chapter of her life: retiring from her medical practice.

As a single woman with no children, she had grown accustomed to living in her four thousand square foot home and doing many of the repairs herself, but the ongoing maintenance and gardening were beginning to impede on the little free time she had. She was ready to retire and downsize her home but was afraid to make such a life change. So we started with the first two guideposts of the Smart Risk Investing Roadmap, identifying her purpose and key people in her circle of trust.

I asked her what she saw as her top financial goals and the *purpose* for the money she had saved. Dr. Ellen's priority was maintaining a secure retirement income so she could completely retire from medicine and have the freedom to travel, write books, and live independently as long as possible.

I then asked her about the most trusted *people* in her circle of trust. In addition to her sister, a few close friends, and me, her financial advisor, she highly respected the counsel of her long-time accountant. With her agreement, I worked with her accountant to come up with a comprehensive view of Dr. Ellen's current and retirement financial picture.

We recommended that she sell her home and downsize to one without stairs. We also advised switching her investments to earn income, as opposed to being tied up in illiquid assets, especially since she had no heirs. She owned a lot of low-interest-paying term deposits and could benefit by moving them into more of a dividend-paying investment strategy.

For Dr. Ellen, it was about working together with people who knew her situation best. She was busy with her work and looking after others, so she never paid attention to her own affairs. But I worked with her accountant to help her see the big picture from a Smart Risk perspective, seeing new options from an objective mind-set, without being blinded by fear of the unknown. By mapping out her various retirement scenarios and showing her the potential risks and rewards of each one, together we were able to formulate a suitable plan to help her achieve her goals.

Plan

The third guidepost for getting past financial obstacles is building a plan. While the plan itself will likely become outdated as life takes its unexpected twists and turns, the *process* of planning is invaluable. One of my clients, who served as a high-ranking official in the US military, once told me, "the plan is nothing, but planning is everything." He shared stories and lessons learned as a fighter pilot during the Vietnam War. He never actually followed the flight plan because, in reality, the sky was riddled with bullets from every direction. But the preparation and planning he had done ahead of time to know the course and destination of his flight plan allowed him to successfully perform an evasive maneuver and be able to adapt in the midst of fire. This planning process is fundamental for financial success too.

For couples, it is important to create a unified plan or strategy between spouses or partners. Map out what is important to you and your spouse, and use milestones to mark where you are today relative to where you need to be at different points in five, ten, or twenty years or more from now. Consider building a financial plan and an investment plan, as well as a roadmap or planning tool designed to keep the financial and investment plans in sync over the years and adaptable to your changing life cycle. We will discuss types of financial and investment plans in more depth in chapter 7.

One example of a planning tool designed to keep financial and investment plans in sync is a goals-based reporting tool. We designed one to help Dr. Ellen understand how the financial and investment plans work together and how they related to her. This goals-based reporting tool showed how well the investment plan was working relative to the amount of financial assets she needed to satisfy the goals prioritized in her financial plan.

Many times in our industry, investors and professionals focus solely on rates of return. Everyone typically wants the highest rate of return possible, but when you're looking at whether you can retire how and when you wish, the rate of return is not the only factor, because pursuing a higher return usually means taking a higher risk. Sometimes, prospective clients ask us, "What do you suggest I invest in to earn 8 percent per year return?" We take a different approach.

Using a Smart Risk approach, we help investors consider both the risk and the return. Maybe it's not really about beating the return of a chosen benchmark or index but, rather, the likelihood of outliving your capital due to taking an improper amount of risk. With a proper financial plan, you may be required to think about how much income you will actually require from your financial assets to live the lifestyle you wish to live and then work backward to determine the type of investment portfolio and plan best equipped to get you there.

We helped Dr. Ellen understand the appropriate risk and return targets for her situation by building her a financial plan, an investment plan, and a goals-based reporting tool instead of simply comparing annual rates of return to evaluate her financial progress. Such goals-based reporting shows your current net worth (i.e., plots the value of your investment pool of capital) on a trajectory map and compares it to where it needs to be over the next years so you can sustain your intended lifestyle to life expectancy.

For Dr. Ellen, we used this goals-based reporting tool to frame every financial discussion. Every time we got together, we compared her net worth to the amount she would reasonably need to sustain her lifestyle to see if she was still on track to meet her goals. Having that plan and showing her that she was actually above the range of what she needed in order to be able to live off that income to the age of ninety-five was tremendously rewarding. (I usually project to age ninety or one hundred years for my clients because people are living longer.)

Having that mapped out for her helped Dr. Ellen see she was well positioned to afford to retire. She felt much more at ease when she saw this projection, as opposed to having the intangible goal of targeting a certain numeric rate of return, which in reality, will vary each year.

Perspective

The fourth guidepost is perspective. For this, investors may need a slight shift in their mind-set to overcome the remaining challenges to building or maintaining wealth. The stories we tell ourselves about money and the excuses we make are often rooted in our childhood experiences or something that happened to us earlier in our lives, and they paint how we see ourselves and how we see money.

Money can be a lot like a mirror, often reflecting your state of mind and how you see the world—it is the lens that influences your creativity and your capacity to give and receive. It's like a window into your soul. If you see money as an enabler and you have positive feelings about it and its ability to create freedom and choice, you'll probably be an enabler in other people's lives. But if you see money as something associated with guilt or pain, you will probably make financial choices/decisions that limit your ability to grow wealth.

Let me share a story that illustrates the importance of perspective. Robert is a friend who is a successful consultant to high-net-worth individuals and deals with money all the time. In the past, in his personal life, he spent it all on lavish cars and houses, almost as if he wanted to get rid of it as fast as possible.

Robert is an insightful man, so he did a lot of work to find out why he was living his life this way. It turned out that he was abused as a child and he was given toys and gifts from his parents to make up for the hurt. He grew up associating money with pain. So all his life, even though he made lots of money to feel good about himself, he couldn't hold onto it, because it was painful. He associated money with feeling guilty. Money can be emotional. Reframing your perspective into a healthy and more rational one can enable you to move forward and ultimately make better choices.

Looking at money from a Smart Risk perspective often requires a mind-shift in thinking about money. A Smart Risk perspective involves recognizing our own biases in terms of how we make decisions about money, and then making a conscious effort to apply a sound, rational approach, based on evaluating the likelihood and magnitude of both positive and negative outcomes. Robert, for example, learned to apply a Smart Risk perspective once he identified the root cause of his associating pain with money. He then worked to build a healthier and more balanced outlook on his money choices. In chapter 8 we will explore some of the successful Smart Risk perspectives that some self-made ultra-wealthy investors share.

Positive action

Following the Smart Risk Investing Roadmap through the first four Ps (purpose, people, plan, and perspective) will help you arrive at this fifth and final guidepost: positive action. The biggest challenge for most investors at this stage is that as soon as they approach the edge of their comfort zone, insecurity raises its ugly head.

But what's on the other side? Empowerment. Your Work-Optional Life. Your legacy. This is where the momentum and resilience you have built from blazing along the Smart Risk Investing Roadmap thus far can propel you forward to your goals. Here is where your circle of trust can help drive change from your current state. It begins with changing how people think. Then we see changes in behaviour.

Dr. Ellen called me in a moment of doubt as she was saying good-bye to her patients. She had actually delivered some of these patients with her own hands. In that moment, I reminded her of how she had been my client for almost a decade and how, over the years, we had built out her roadmap and routinely measured her financial progress, which was well on track for her to be able to retire with enough resources. We had survived and thrived after the 2007–2008 crisis, and she was financially ready to begin her Work-Optional Life.

I reminded her of how, years earlier, she had faced similar fears that she successfully overcame, as when we helped her take that step out of her comfort zone to sell her overly conservative investments and invest wisely. There's still always going to be that force trying to pull you back into that comfort zone, so the trick is to recognize it, embrace it, and take that step away from it.

When she called, Dr. Ellen just needed that extra support to confirm that she could take the final step to begin her active retirement. So sometimes it's not just about overcoming the hump once. The Smart Risk Investing Roadmap can help you along an ongoing, dynamic process. People get pulled back in and require that extra nudge every once in a while to help them overcome common obstacles to reaching their financial goals.

Dr. Ellen finally took the step. She mailed out letters to each of her patients informing them of her decision to retire after more than thirty years of family medical practice. Once she began receiving the overwhelming number of letters and phone calls of support and gratitude from her patients, she felt liberated. This happened more than a year ago, and today, she is happier than ever. She is enjoying an active life abundant with travel, gardening, visits with friends, and the freedom to see patients on a locum basis without the stresses of her previous lifestyle.

The Five Ps: Guideposts in action

Allow me to share another story. My client Jessica is a fifty-five-year-old woman who works in the travel industry and splits her time between Canada and the USA. When I met her, she had fallen into a false perception of safety, where she had placed a large inheritance into an account that primarily held bank term deposits, guaranteed investment certificates (GICs) and bonds. Because the interest rates she was earning were so low, she was selling portions of the original capital to cover her living expenses, but she was depleting her capital quickly. She had not yet realized the *purpose* for her money. The wrong *people* also surrounded her in her circle of trust. She needed people who could advise her to put herself in a better position, especially because she didn't have a steady source of income from her work or her investments.

Jessica was selling GICs and living off the cash. One of her good friends, who is one of my clients, recognized that this was not sustainable for her. He feared that in the not-too-distant future, Jessica would run out of capital and have no choices left. He asked me if I would be willing to meet with Jessica and offer her some help. When I met with Jessica, it became clear to me that the main purpose for her money was to ensure she did not outlive her capital. As a single woman in a career with no pension, I helped her realize she was spending it too quickly to realize her purpose.

Next, we helped build her a suitable *plan*. I showed her an illustration of how little retirement income she would have left if she continued to live off the principal from her guaranteed investment term deposits. I compared this to a couple of alternative customized investment approaches that might work better for her over the long run.

As part of the plan, I gave her choices. I showed her what it would look like if she moved into a different type of asset mix and walked her through the pros and cons of each alternative. I wanted to turn her away from her perception of safety to a much better and safer situation where she would be living less off the capital and more on the investment income.

Her change in *perspective* began with recognizing her underlying beliefs about money and investing. It turned out that she had, from a young age, seen her father living with a fixed pension plan, back when interest rates were much higher. Her father was conservative. He was a professor and owned very conservative investments all his life.

Growing up, she never really had to make a lot of financial decisions, so when her father passed away and she received this small inheritance, she was on her own. Her natural tendency was to do the most conservative thing. Her monetary belief was that she would always be provided for; she would always have an income.

Shedding light on her belief about money and how it was affecting her ability to make better decisions helped her move forward. It took some time for her to be willing to accept some smarter risks and proactive action. After several meetings with Jessica, my team and I helped her transition to a more flexible and appropriate investment portfolio that was designed to help her wealth grow and sustain her lifestyle.

We helped Jessica move from a false perception of safety to a much better position, and now she has accumulated and built a much larger critical mass of assets and a deeper pool of capital to draw on as she approaches her retirement. By applying the Smart Risk Investing Roadmap, we helped Jessica identify her purpose, build a stronger advisory team and circle of trust, establish a more suitable financial and investment plan, shift her overly conservative perspective, and ultimately, take positive action to reshape her investment portfolio. She took a good risk, a Smart Risk.

SUMMARY

Consider the Smart Risk Investing Roadmap to help move past challenges to building wealth and achieving financial freedom:

- *Purpose*. Begin with the end in mind. List and rank your goals for your financial resources.
- *People*. Surround yourself with the right people to help you make smart decisions. Investing success depends a lot on the intelligence, temperament, and judgment of the people managing it.
- *Plan***.** Develop a suitable financial plan and investment plan that can be measured along the way to enable you to enjoy a sustainable lifestyle in retirement, as opposed to being focused simply on a rate of return or fear of losing money.
- *Perspective*, Be open-minded to changing your perspective and taking action that breaks through the emotional baggage holding you back.
- *Positive action*. Use the momentum from cruising past the first four guideposts, and take the next step toward achieving your financial goals.

QUESTIONS

1. What is the number-one challenge holding you back from reaching your full financial potential?
2. Which guidepost (purpose, people, plan, perspective, positive action) within the Smart Risk Investing Roadmap could you help move closer to your financial potential today?
3. Who are the most valuable members of your own circle of trust? Who would you like to add to your own circle of trust? Why?
4. What are the potential blind spots in your current financial or investment plan, and how might you address the identified gaps?
5. What change in perspective—or personal bias—might enable you to take a step in a different, much healthier financial direction?
6. What is one positive action step you can take today that would further improve your financial situation?

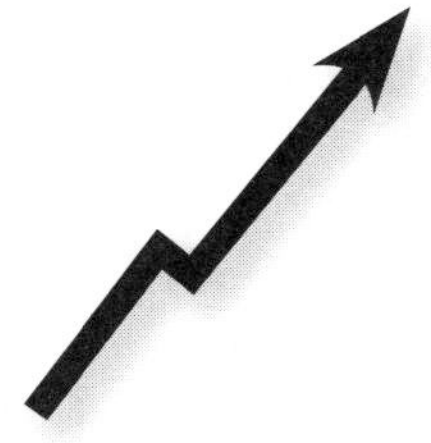

CHAPTER 5

Purpose: Defining Your Purpose for Wealth and the Work-Optional Life

A master in the art of living draws no sharp distinction between his work and his play, his mind and his body, his education and his recreation. He hardly knows which is which. He simply pursues his vision or excellence through whatever he is doing and leaves others to determine whether he is working or playing. To himself, he always seems to be doing both.

—Lawrence Pearsall Jacks

Starting with why

Why do you need wealth? The answer to that question frames the whole concept of defining your purpose for money, the first guidepost in the Smart Risk Investing Roadmap. For some, the goal of building wealth is to create a life completely independent of work, enabling them to enjoy an active retirement. I call this a Work-Optional Life. But for some, there is more to it. Many of my clients have more than enough to live on in retirement, but they still have a drive to keep building wealth.

Is it for the next generation? To create a lasting legacy? To make a contribution toward making the world a better place for your family or for the community in which you live? In a recent study done in America by US Trust, which surveyed 640 wealthy investors with over $3 million in investible assets, excluding the value of their home, a surprising few—only about one third—felt they were prepared to achieve their most important family needs and goals.

A similarly low number responded that they felt prepared for the thing that's really on their mind: living longer lifespans. Does this imply that $3 million investible assets, today, are not enough for a comfortable retirement at current standards? Perhaps it reflects that having more money raises more complex issues. According to the study, wealthy investors indeed want more and have complex purposes for their money. They care deeply about philanthropy, elder-care planning, and teaching their children financial skills. What is your main purpose for building wealth?

Creating a legacy or creating more problems?

According to this same study, while many wealthy Americans want to leave an inheritance to their children, only 25 percent strongly agree that their children are prepared to inherit the family wealth. And while most of these affluent parents say their family would benefit from establishing a set of guiding principles to guide the purpose of their wealth, only 10 percent have actually done so. In fact, almost two thirds of wealthy parents have said little or nothing about the family wealth to their children, and most cite their concern that it will affect their children's work ethic as the reason. If creating a legacy is important to you, what are you doing today to enable this besides leaving a lump sum of money when you are gone?

Active retirement

Many of my clients' primary purpose in building wealth is to secure a comfortable and active retirement, enjoy a high quality of life, and leave a meaningful contribution when they're gone. Often, clients in early retirement today enjoy "active travel," including visits to developing countries, historic ruins, or even safaris to parts of the world they have not yet explored. Curiosity about the world around them has created growing demand for options such as river cruises, which offer travelers the intimate experience of sailing on small ships to exclusive destinations via rivers and waterways throughout Europe, the Mediterranean, South East Asia, and Africa.

The Work-Optional Life

How would you feel if you didn't have to worry about showing up to work every morning or paying your bills? What would it feel like if you could freely live your life and travel anywhere in the world? How would it feel to know you could start any new venture you could dream of without worrying about earning an income? Or that you could create a legacy for others to remember you by, generations from now?

I hope you're now really thinking about the benefits of a Work-Optional Life. A Work-Optional Life is a way of living whereby you don't have to work for an income, because your investment portfolio is now working for you and generating sustainable income for life, giving you true financial freedom.

You are then able to pursue other activities and interests and continue to work only if you choose to. Why would you choose to stay active or still "go to work" if you didn't have to earn a living? It's simple, and many people do it. Doing what you love can provide great satisfaction in terms of the following:

- feeling productive
- enjoying challenging activities
- providing a sense of service
- creating a sense of contribution
- rewarding both the ego and others by making use of your experience
- staying mentally and physically fit

For many, achieving and maintaining a Work-Optional Life is the number-one priority and purpose for building wealth. Having spent my career working with highly successful, self-made, wealthy investors who are enjoying being Work-Optional, I've learned that reaching this goal is the result of strong financial management processes and taking Smart Risks all along the way.

OLD definition of retirement	WORK-OPTIONAL definition of retirement
Retirement is an ending	Life balance
Relief from work	Renewing old passions
No work means no growth	Sense of authentic self
Reliance on others	Life enrichment
Passive, monotonous, boring	Self-esteem
No more decisions to make	Involvement
No schedules to keep	Exploration

The leaky bucket

Let's consider, for a moment, a leaky bucket as a tool for visualizing the balancing act of maintaining a Work-Optional Life. The bucket holds all the wealth you have accumulated to date. You want the bucket to be brimming with financial assets or at least reach a certain critical mass so that all of the accumulated "stuff" in the bucket can help sustain you through retirement. Going into that bucket over the years is what you make from your income, inheritances, investment returns, and any other sources of money.

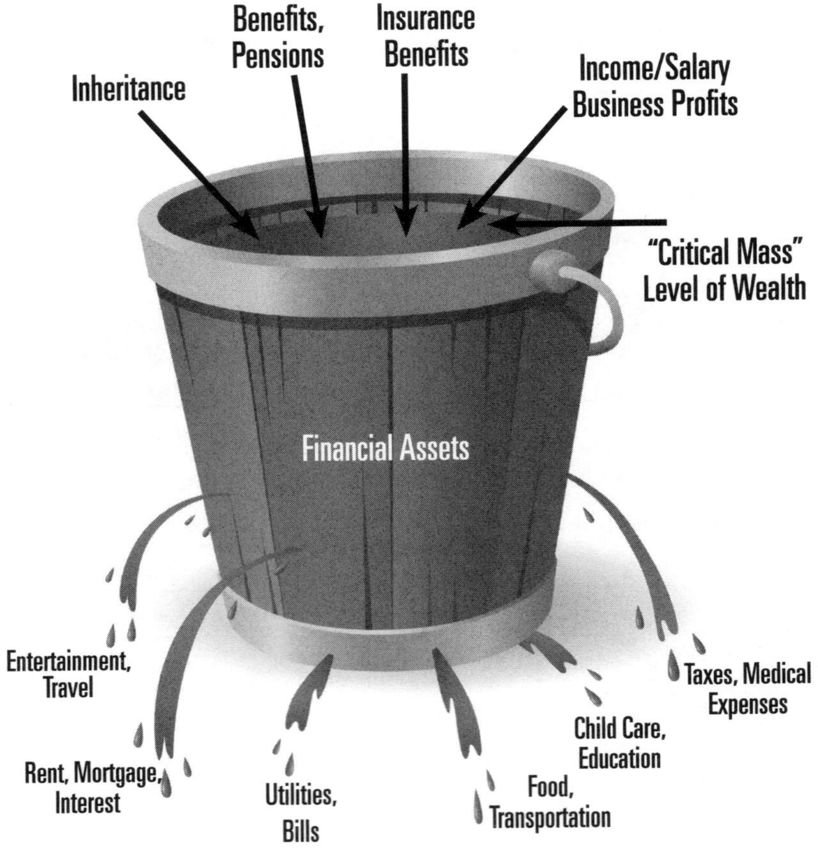

But your bucket has a lot of holes. It's a leaky bucket. One of those holes represents what leaks out in taxes. Another hole represents expenses and spending on groceries, bills, bottles of wine, rent, or mortgage payments. There are many holes. Once you've visualized your own leaky bucket, ask yourself, "Which holes can be plugged first?"

The goal is to increase the level of financial assets in your bucket to reach a critical mass. In order to increase what's in that bucket, three things can happen: (1) you earn more money, which is sometimes difficult; (2) you can plug the holes in the bucket; (3) you have what's *in the bucket* growing at a faster rate—and that's where financial and investment planning comes in.

Once you are able to manage and balance the inflows and outflows and keep your assets at or above the "critical mass" level, you will be well on your way to achieving the Work-Optional Life.

The critical mass line: a moving target

Good financial planning and investment success can help you achieve the Work-Optional Life, but don't be surprised if that critical mass level keeps moving higher. The critical mass level often creeps higher as lifestyles evolve. Many smart, rational investors are still surprised at how much more they actually needed in their bucket in order to sustain their active retirement.

Let me share a story about a client named Peter, who is in his early sixties. Peter loves to fish in the tropics. He and his wife moved to Canada when he was twenty-two years old. He was successful working in the finance industry and owning his own company. His goal back then was to retire with enough capital to live off risk-free investments with no worries. But in reality, the amount of capital that he thought he might need—$1 million—was short of the multiple millions he feels he needs today.

Forty years ago, $1 million was a lot of money. In reality, even $5 million may not be enough to sustain his active lifestyle today. But back then, thinking about saving enough to have $5 million in retirement would have been almost impossible for him to fathom.

About twenty years ago, he wisely realized he would have to accept risk later on in life to accommodate his goal. Things have changed—

this low-interest-rate environment, for instance. Even in 2009–2011, everyone thought it would just be a matter of time before economies got back to normal, meaning much higher interest rates. So he realized that in order to achieve the income he needed, he had to accept more risk.

Peter moved to Canada forty years ago with $304 in his pocket. He worked hard, was successful, and always stayed focused on his goal to save up a critical mass of assets so he would be able to stop working. Early on, he thought he knew how much capital he required and how much risk he was willing to take, but what he didn't anticipate were the changing economic environment and the higher cost and standard of living he and his wife would become accustomed to over the decades.

Today, at age sixty-two, he has accepted that he needs to take Smart Risks and maintain investments in real estate and equities to fund his lifestyle. He also says he needs to have people like me to manage the day-to-day investment decisions for him so that he can still enjoy his lifestyle. He knows he needs to be invested, but instead of micromanaging his investments, he would rather spend his time travelling, writing books, and fishing in the tropics.

During the 2007–2008 financial crisis, Peter was able to set emotions aside and invest in companies that were paying good dividends. It was a scary time for most people, but having been an entrepreneur with an acceptance of risk in his blood, he had the deep-rooted sense that he should take advantage of a crisis. So he learned to stop, turn off the TV, and look at the balance sheets of the companies in which he was considering investing. Instead of being a "headline investor," he became a "balance sheet investor."

Today he has a multimillion portfolio of both real estate and equity investments. He and his wife freely travel, and we make sure he is able to continue living a successful and active Work-Optional Life.

My journey to finding my purpose

Looking back, working amongst the elite investment team at Eton Park Capital in New York City represented the pinnacle of what I had sought to achieve in my career. So why did I resign and choose instead to move back to Vancouver, British Columbia? The success felt hollow. Something was missing for me. It was not until years later that I found out what it was.

New York, my career, and my achievements had become my identity, my comfort zone for years. Yet, I was not getting anywhere in my search for happiness and the Work-Optional Life that I had envisioned for myself. I was working myself to the bone, but for whom? For what purpose? The ripples of the 9/11 crisis years earlier had quietly had their impact on me, putting my life in perspective. It was time for me to take a step outside my comfort zone, take a risk—a Smart Risk—and build my own investment business, on my own terms.

> Today, I have built a successful wealth management practice with my mentor, my father. We are the principals of a multigenerational wealth advisory family business that combines the expertise of our diverse schools of financial thought, and the synergies of our multi-faceted investment backgrounds to bring valued solutions to our clients, relieving them of financial stresses and helping them achieve their goals sooner.

My purpose

Over the years I've done a lot of thinking about what's important to me and why I get up every day to go to work. I help my clients realize the purpose for their money, empowering them to live better lives. I have an exponential impact on something beyond myself.

I enjoy being a catalyst for my clients. In chemistry, a catalyst is just a small, relatively insignificant ingredient in the overall equation. But through the catalyst's participation and contribution, the bigger outcome can be quite magnificent and enduring. That's what gets me excited. That's why I love what I do.

The loss and the rebirth

The losses I witnessed people experience in the 2007–2008 financial crisis gave me a sense of renewed purpose. It motivated my father and me to step up our efforts to build an investment strategy that safeguards investors' portfolios to prevent that kind of disaster from happening to them again. I call this the Wealth Catalyst Investment Process™ and we will discuss it in chapter 7. I became even further compelled to educate investors on how to recognize behavioural biases and overcome emotional mistakes to prevent them from straying from that sound investment strategy.

The sandwich generation

Let me share a story about my client Barbara, a successful realtor. We helped her achieve her purpose of living a Work-Optional Life. She is a member of what I call the sandwich generation, supporting her mother who lives in Asia and her daughters and grandchildren who live throughout Canada and the USA. Barbara's not actively working anymore. Instead, she's doing what she loves, which includes playing golf and travelling. Over the past ten years, by following the Smart Risk Investing Roadmap, we've been able to help her build the financial assets in her leaky bucket so we can now generate steady investment income for her. She doesn't have to worry about selling homes anymore. She's been receiving $8,000 every month from her investment portfolio for years, and the value of that portfolio continues to rise.

Working professionals can achieve the Work-Optional Life too

Another example is a younger working couple, Jeremy and his partner. They're in their midfifties now. They met me while they were in their forties, and both were salaried workers who did a great job of saving a portion of their earnings every year through an automatic savings programme.

But instead of staying safe in conservative cash-like investments, they actively took Smart Risks, both before, during, and after the 2007–2008 financial crisis. We guided them through a full financial and investment planning process and built a goals-based reporting tool and leaky bucket tool, which showed what they would need to sustain their anticipated annual income goal in retirement.

But they kept raising the amount they needed to live on because their travel tastes kept escalating. This caused us to raise the critical mass level of their leaky bucket, which in turn led us to update their financial and investment plans to tilt toward more growth so they could still be successful in achieving their desired retirement income.

The critical mass level of your leaky bucket is a moving target, and it's more and more important to have a suitable and adaptable investment plan that adjusts to your changing needs and goals.

Jeremy and his partner's goal was to retire at the age of fifty-five. They both were willing to work longer but, ideally, wanted to stop and live off their assets with a projected $100,000 combined income after tax. Today, as a result of following the Smart Risk Investing Roadmap and achieving solid investment results, Jeremy and his partner are on track to begin enjoying their Work-Optional Life together. This shows that planning is not just for the ultra-wealthy. Salaried employees can and should do it too, but they should be prepared to start early, be diligent with their savings, and also be willing to take Smart Risks along the way.

SUMMARY

- Understand your motivators, your *why* for building wealth.
- Consider the magnitude or scope of the influence you want to have with the wealth you are building. How much of an impact do you really want to have? Is it just for your lifetime, for your family, for your community, for your country? Is it greater?
- Achieving and maintaining a Work-Optional Life is all about starting early, getting the right advice, and having a resilient investment strategy to stay on track when life throws you obstacles. Consider the Smart Risk Investing Roadmap and the Five Ps to accelerate your ability to overcome obstacles to achieving your Work-Optional Life.
- Meet with your advisor on a regular basis to ensure your purpose is properly reflected in your plans.
- Visualize or illustrate your own financial leaky bucket and consider how you might reach and maintain the critical mass level sooner.

QUESTIONS

1. What does your vision of financial success look like and why?
2. What legacy would you want your wealth to have today? In the future?
3. If you never had to work again—if you enjoyed a completely Work-Optional Life—how would you spend your days?
4. What are the biggest holes in your own leaky bucket, and what is your critical mass level?
5. How might you reach your critical mass level sooner (i.e., plug holes, increase what's going into your bucket, or help increase the rate of growth of the assets within in your bucket)?

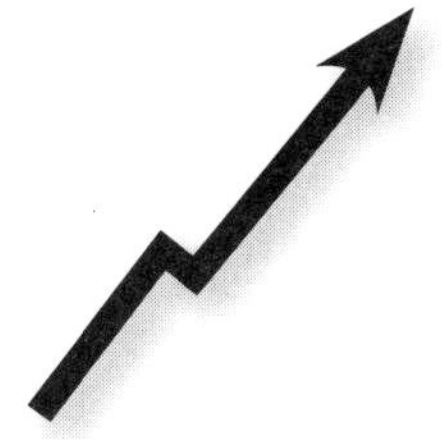

CHAPTER 6

People: The Value of Your Circle of Trust, Especially Beyond Active Retirement

Friends are sometimes a big help when they share your feelings. In the context of decisions, the friends who serve you best are those who understand your feelings but are not overly impressed by them.
—Daniel Kahneman, *Thinking Fast and Slow*

It's an exciting time to be facing retirement today. Thirty-five years ago, life expectancy for a sixty-five-year-old male was eighty, and for a female, it was eighty-four. Now it's even higher. According to the Canadian Institute of Actuaries, in 2014, 25 percent of sixty-five-year-old women and 17 percent of sixty-five-year-old men lived past the age of ninety-five. For financial planning, we used to project out to eighty-five. Now we're projecting out to ninety-five or even one hundred, so we can show a realistic projection of whether people will outlive their capital.

Unfortunately, our Canadian and US pension systems weren't designed to keep up with people living this long beyond their working years. Two generations ago, people used to work almost until they couldn't. But now, people are living twenty or thirty, sometimes forty years beyond their working life, and under the current low-interest-rate environment and bulging retirement populations draining the stressed system, people need to have their own independent retirement plan. They also need a team of trusted people in their circle of trust to ensure the plan is relevant and executed as intended.

Circle of trust

Consider building an A team, a personal board of directors, a scrum, a wolf pack or mastermind group of people with different skill sets, who are both highly competent and aligned in helping you achieve your most important goals. This "Jedi council" may open your mind-set to new and productive ideas. But it's not enough just to have these people around you. Introduce them to each other so they can operate and communicate as a cohesive team when necessary.

I often play the role of "scrum master" for my clients, or "quarterback," to facilitate communication and alignment amongst the professionals and key people in my clients' circle of trust. Individual members in your circle may change and evolve over time, and below is an example of the types of skill sets and people you may want to have in your circle. Having this safety net can be particularly invaluable as you age and as your needs become more complex, even if you are not able to see it yourself.

The Circle of Trust™

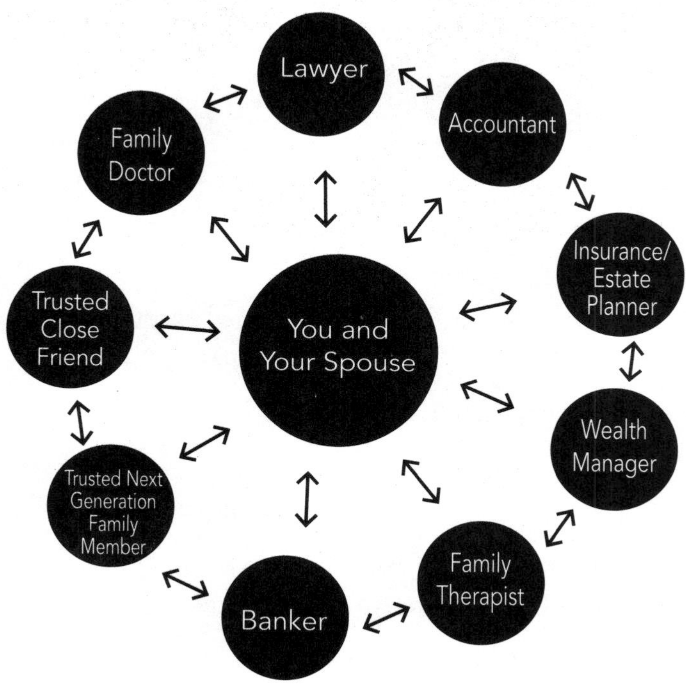

Victor and Nancy: an unexpected roadblock

Let me share with you what happened to Victor and Nancy. One day in 2011, during one of our regular financial review meetings, Victor and Nancy appeared uneasy. Nancy explained that Victor had developed a form of dementia, and she needed help. She loved Victor, and while she no longer could physically care for him alone, she knew that he wanted to stay in the comfort of their home, so she asked us for help.

The first step I took was to ensure that they had the right people in their circle of trust, which included their trusted tax accountant, legal advisor, their medical doctor, two of their sons, and me. I planned a meeting for us all to meet in my boardroom, along with Victor and Nancy. Those who couldn't join us in the meeting attended by way of a conference call to ensure we were on the same page regarding their next stage in life.

Next, to make Victor and Nancy's updated goals financially viable, I presented the idea of generating additional investment income to pay for full-time home care. Both Victor and Nancy liked this idea. So I built an investment plan designed to provide sustainable monthly dividends and income that would send the cash straight to their bank accounts each month.

It started with one home care aid, but as Victor's mental and physical health declined, the need escalated to three full-time home care aids. It was expensive. Over the years since we began managing their investments, we managed to grow their wealth to satisfy their objectives, compounding their growth back above where they started before the global financial crisis. From their roughly $3 million investment portfolio we were able to start them off with $3,000 a month and slowly increase the amount to $8,000 a month. Nancy was very grateful that we had enabled her to give Victor the best life he could enjoy until his final days.

Victor passed away peacefully two years later, in 2013. Thankfully, we had helped to establish a strong circle of trust around Nancy. So she was well looked after with a strong support network to help work through the estate and probate process, allowing her to grieve and find a way forward.

It's not just about how long people live; it's about quality of life. When you begin to lose control, having the right *people* around you can help you continue to enjoy life as you had intended.

Dementia-proofing your portfolio

It can be a delicate subject, but it needs to be addressed, as cognitive decline among people nearing or in retirement is growing dramatically. In the USA, approximately one in eight retired baby boomers suffers from dementia or cognitive impairment, with two million new cases reported every year, according to research done by Harvard University. More than 40 percent over the age of 80 have dementia, and almost 70 percent are cognitively impaired, researchers say, and the numbers are similar in Canada.

Life often throws unanticipated curve balls. While you cannot change what may happen to you or your loved ones, you can do your best to be prepared for the unexpected. Dementia-proofing your portfolio is one way to prepare for the possibility of you or your loved one suffering serious mental decline, so your care and finances will be managed in a straightforward and carefully planned manner. Here is where applying the Smart Risk Investing Roadmap and using the Five Ps (particularly people, plan, and shifting from the perspective that "it won't happen to me") can help overcome the challenges of living a healthy active retirement.

The costs of care

According to Statistics Canada, there is about a 10 percent chance of needing some sort of long-term-care assistance by age fifty-five, about a 30 percent chance by age sixty-five, and a 50 percent chance by age seventy-five. These costs have a huge impact on a couple's retirement. As an example, the cost to live in a private nursing home in British Columbia, Canada, can range from $1,000 to $3,000 per month, whereas the cost to live in a retirement home (for more independent living) in British Columbia can cost $6,000 or more per month and even more when you add services. The cost varies considerably across provinces.

There are key differences between long-term-care facilities, otherwise known as nursing homes and retirement homes.

A long-term-care facility, or nursing home, provides accommodation for people who require on-site supervised care twenty-four hours a day, seven days a week. For the most part, these residents are not able to look after themselves and in many cases, require extensive care services. Since long-term-care facilities are subsidized by the government in Canada, their staff-to-resident ratios are carefully managed. To be eligible for a nursing home, the candidate has to be assessed by a doctor and go through an evaluation process.

A retirement home, on the other hand, offers suites for seniors within a more independent environment where they have the flexibility to come and go as they please. The basic services are, generally, included in the monthly costs—for example, housekeeping and freshly prepared meals. As residents require more services and health-related support, these can often be provided at the retirement home "a la carte" for additional fees. However, not every retirement home offers additional support services.

On the next page is a table summarizing the private cost of long-term care in Canada.

	Retirement homes/ residences		Nursing homes	
	$ Yearly Cost		$ Yearly Cost	
Province	Minimum	Maximum	Minimum	Maximum
Alberta	12,000	65,000	18,100	22,100
BC	13,000	70,000	11,650	37,100
Manitoba	15,000	42,000	12,400	28,900
New Brunswick	9,600	54,000	N/A	41,250
Newfoundland	20,100	50,000		33,600
Nova Scotia	23,000	72,000	22,500	38,000
Ontario	14,000	132,000	20,800	29,300
Prince Edward Island	7,200	63,000	N/A	28,300
Quebec	6,000	42,000	13,100	21,100
Saskatchewan	16,600	60,000	12,600	23,900

The Private Cost of Long-Term Care in Canada
Source: Senioropolis Inc., 2014

There is no Canada-wide standardization with respect to either retirement or nursing homes. Each province uses slightly different terminology and may not include the same criteria in their pricing. These numbers are directional only and should not be used for planning or budgeting.

Early signs of cognitive decline

Often the key lies in recognizing these early signs of cognitive decline in spouses and loved ones, as they themselves are not likely to point them out. The National Endowment for Financial Education has compiled a helpful checklist of early warning signs that may indicate when an older adult's financial competence is declining. Consider sharing this list with the people you have chosen to surround you in your circle of trust. The list on the next page is based on research conducted by Dr. Daniel Marson of the University of Alabama in Birmingham.

Warning signs of cognitive decline

1. Taking longer to complete everyday financial tasks:
   - taking longer than usual to
     - prepare bills for mailing
     - fill out a check
2. Reduced attention to details in financial documents:
   - having trouble
     - identifying an overdue bill that needs attention
     - finding specific details in a bank statement
3. Decline in everyday math skills:
   - having trouble
     - calculating a return on an investment
     - figuring out a tip in a restaurant
4. Difficulty identifying risks in a financial opportunity:
   - having trouble
     - identifying the key risk in an investment scenario
     - understanding the risks of mail or telephone fraud

Dementia-proofing against financial fraud

Let me share a story about one of my client's experience with dementia. Maria is a seventy-five-year-old retiree who received a phone call from her nephew, desperate for her help. Maria's brother, Phil, had been acting strangely and was threatening to remove his son's (her nephew's) power of attorney because Phil thought his son was meddling in his financial affairs.

Phil was in his eighties and residing in a retirement community, living off a large cash balance of term deposits and short-term GICs held on bank deposit. When Maria went to visit Phil at her nephew's request, she found three large boxes of letters Phil had collected. They all requested money to be sent in the mail to a suspicious sweep-stakes, claiming Phil had won a large cash prize that could only be collected after he sent a check of $50 or $500 or $5,000. To her horror, after investigating the situation with her nephew, they found Phil had not even realized that he had sent over $300,000 in a series of more than three hundred checks to an out-of-country address over the previous six months. Phil had been suffering from dementia but had refused to get help.

In another situation, a fellow advisor worked with his elderly client to help ward off financial fraud within her own family. Agatha was an eighty-five-year-old widow whose two nephews and sole beneficiaries lived in another province. Sadly, one of Agatha's nephews was constantly in need of money. He played on her emotions and soon had her requesting amounts in the tens of thousands to be drawn from her investment portfolio to give to him. Her financial advisor thought twice before sending out the large checks and called Agatha's trusted friend and power of attorney, Carolyn, to discuss the matter.

Agatha's advisor and Carolyn both had noticed the deterioration in Agatha's ability to comprehend financial matters, including her ability to calculate the tip at the restaurant where they frequently met for lunch. Together, they called Agatha, who remembered nothing about the call requesting funds, and then they called the nephew. These calls from both Agatha's advisor and her power of attorney were enough to scare the nephew from victimizing Agatha again and are a testament to the value of Agatha building her circle of trust well in advance.

Sometimes, the obstacle in your roadmap can become your own deteriorating cognitive abilities. *Plan* with trusted advisors—your powers of attorney, financial advisor, executors, loved ones, and other *people* within your circle of trust—how the investments should be managed to follow through with your intended objectives if you are no longer able to manage things. Also try to include your spouse in these meetings, especially when one of you tends to make most of the financial decisions. If one spouse has, traditionally, been in charge of the finances, the other needs to be educated about money, budgeting, risk, and investments.

The next step is to ease the move through this difficult shift in *perspective*. There can be a lot of fear and denial over losing one's mental or cognitive functions; we simply think it won't happen to us. So try to develop a Plan B, just in case.

Lastly, work toward *positive action* by doing comprehensive estate planning with your financial advisor, and get your legal documents in place. It's important that you update your will, have living wills in place, and appoint powers of attorney who can step in and act on your behalf when needed, as in Agatha's case. Proactive estate planning is imperative, as this may also include discussing insurance plans, investment management style, long-term-care provisions, and tax planning.

For one client, Professor Lee, the problem wasn't dementia; it was cancer. She was a single, highly educated, retired professor with no children. When she was diagnosed with cancer, we phoned her and tried to make sure she had somebody to look after her. She was released from the hospital because she was in her eighties and considered no longer treatable.

We wanted to see if there was anybody who could look after her. She did have some friends and a power of attorney, so we invited her power of attorney, who was her niece, and Professor Lee, to a meeting with us to talk about how she wanted her affairs to be handled. We made sure everybody was on the same page. She passed away a couple of months later.

We had a long relationship with Professor Lee, so we had the benefit of understanding her true priorities. By establishing communication with her power of attorney and developing a plan together, we were able to have everything in order so the power of attorney knew where everything was and how to proceed. Otherwise, it might have been a more difficult and longer estate process for her family.

"Wellness and Financial Care" binder

Another client, Cheryl, is in her nineties and, for the past ten years since her husband passed away, has been on her own and living off the income from her investment portfolio that we help manage. During the 2007–2008 financial crisis, Cheryl had been worried that her investment income might be in jeopardy. I met with Cheryl and her daughter to provide leadership and confidence in the planning we had designed to withstand the volatility. Sure enough, before, during, and after the crisis, and even to this day, her monthly distribution from her investment portfolio has never gone down. In fact, it's gone up.

But we took it one step further. For her additional peace of mind, we built Cheryl a "Wellness and Financial Care" binder that serves as a place to document and update her personal and financial information so that all of her important information can be found in one place. It contains not only her important contact information but also her medical background, financial information, where to find her safe deposit box, insurance policies, and latest will and serves as a handy guide when talking with health-care providers, financial and legal advisors, executors, family members, and others within her circle of trust.

SUMMARY

- The costs of living beyond the active years of retirement can be staggering, especially now, as a greater share of the responsibility has shifted from employers and government to the individual.
- The increasing occurrence of dementia and cognitive decline is something we all need to consider. Look for any early warning signals, and be ready with the right plans in place.
- Be wary of financial fraud targeting the elderly, and build a strong and familiar relationship with your advisor to withstand monetary requests made by predatory or mentally unstable sources.
- Having the right advocates in your circle of trust is of utmost importance, particularly when you are living beyond your active years in retirement.
- Consider creating a "Wellness and Financial Care" binder to keep important information readily available for when it's needed most.

QUESTIONS

1. How do you envision your needs being met beyond your active retirement years?
2. If the ideal situation were not 100 percent achievable, what would be an acceptable and realistic Plan B for you as you age and your care needs increase?
3. What conversations might you have today—and with whom—to prepare for a time where you may not be cognitively fit to make important decisions?
4. Are there significant gaps in your financial and investment plans if you can no longer make sound financial decisions for yourself?
5. Who relies on you for your financial assistance? What can you do today to help prepare them to be better equipped—without you—should that time ever come?

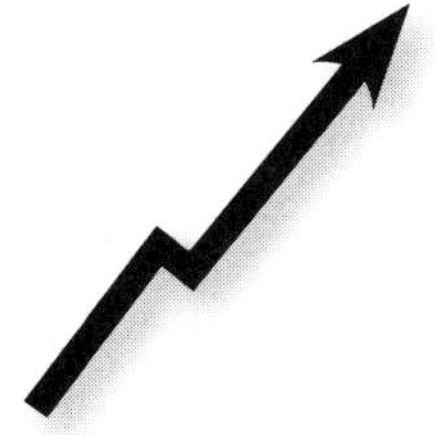

CHAPTER 7

Plan: Resilient Financial and Investment Strategies to Get You to Your Goal

To invest successfully does not require a stratospheric IQ, unusual business insights, or inside information. What's needed is a sound intellectual framework for making decisions, and the ability to keep emotions from corroding the framework.
—Warren Buffett

An integral element in the Smart Risk Investing Roadmap is the plan. Today more than ever before, a disciplined and adaptable investment plan or strategy is required to overcome the myriad of challenges investors face. The traditional strategy of buy and hold, a 60/40 mix of stocks and bonds, failed to withstand the whipsaws and volatility of the financial crises of the past two decades, as many investors succumbed to fear and anxiety, selling at losses and crushing their retirement nest eggs. Investors today need a strategy that works in volatile markets.

Borne out of the strife investors faced after the wrath of September 11, 2001, and the pain they experienced in 2007–2008, a new quest arose for risk-adjusted returns and authentically balanced portfolios. This is why we embrace an investment philosophy that weaves together both the science and art of investing, combining both man and machine, both bottom-up fundamentals and top-down analysis in an active investment approach designed to provide long-term sustainable income and growth in portfolios so investors can have more control over how they live in retirement.

Consider a strategy that takes a Smart Risk approach to investing, using a disciplined process of rational and fact-based decision making to continually stack the odds of investment success in your favour, even in volatile markets.

It starts with the financial plan

There are investment strategies, and there are also financial planning strategies. Consider an orchestra. I used to enjoy regularly attending orchestral performances at Carnegie Hall in New York, and the conductor always mesmerized me. The conductor listens to the music and understands the technical parts of each instrument's role, but at the same time, in his head he hears the music a couple of beats ahead so he can lead all the different instruments playing different melodies and harmonies into one beautiful resonating sound from the entire orchestra. The conductor is incredibly brilliant at weaving together the art and science of the complex symphony to pull off a musical masterpiece. If a musician falls off beat, the conductor is able to lead him back on track.

This analogy speaks to how investors can benefit from having an experienced "conductor" anticipate and orchestrate the financial planning and investment planning techniques required to invest successfully over the long term. As financial advisors, we are always trying to navigate shifts in the complex investment world, at the same time being aware of our clients' changing personal financial situations. These are two completely independent melodies that we weave into one beautiful harmony. As does the conductor, we're also trying to think two steps ahead. So first, we help clients build a financial plan.

A financial plan provides direction to financial decisions and projects what future net worth, cash flow, and retirement income may look like under certain assumptions. The components of financial planning include, but are not limited to, the following:

1. Financial statement preparation and analysis
2. Net worth planning
3. Income tax planning
4. Family and education planning
5. Insurance planning and risk management
6. Retirement income planning
7. Estate planning

For example, creating Victor and Nancy's financial plan was an illuminating exercise. Early in our relationship, while Victor was still working in his practice, the couple had enjoyed spending freely without any real budgeting. But when I asked them to project how much spending they might require in retirement, they looked at each other in puzzlement. They had never felt the need to budget their spending in the past, so they didn't have an estimate of what they would need in the future.

After taking them through a full discovery process that involved digging deeper into their spending, saving, and financial patterns, we were able to calculate and project their future cash flow needs and show them a few different scenarios. These scenarios painted a realistic picture of what their future retirement picture might look like, along with a more pessimistic case and a more optimistic case. These scenarios helped me frame and prioritize discussions and action steps with Victor and Nancy over the next few years.

Making it automatic

I have built hundreds of financial plans for clients over the years, and one simple strategy I often recommend to clients is to set up an automatic savings deposit plan. Set up automatic transfers from your bank account to your investments to take place each month, and increase the amount once or twice per year. How much should you be saving from their income? The more the better, as the goal is to accelerate the growth of the assets in your leaky bucket. Often we recommend aiming for at least 10 percent to 20 percent of your pre-tax income. Pay yourself first, and you'll appreciate it later.

The key is to start early. The power of that money fueling the portfolio and compounding over time provides you with the ability to seize opportunities if there is a downturn in the market. With cash to deploy at bargain-price levels, you can turn volatility into your advantage.

The importance of updating the financial plan

When Victor passed away a few years later, Nancy needed our help to pick up the pieces of her life and adjust to her new circumstances. They had been married for forty-five years, and she had spent the previous three years focused on attending to him and his deteriorating mental condition. She didn't remember what it was like to be on her own, let alone be in the driver's seat of her financial situation. So we took her back to the basics.

Having helped clients survive and thrive in previous financial crises like the one in 2007–2008, and remembering the despair I had felt when I was homeless and alone after September 11, 2001, I was determined to not let Nancy fall. Wanting her to succeed, I walked her through the financial planning process all over again, but this time taking into consideration her own priorities for sustaining a Work-Optional Life and leaving a legacy to her grandchildren.

Next, the investment plan

Many investors have a financial plan that shows what they need to meet their goals but lack a resilient investment plan that effectively shows how to build or preserve wealth to meet the goals set out in their financial plan.

On the investment planning side, it can be challenging for investors to take all the complex knowledge of the financial markets and convert it into simple steps they can apply to achieving financial security and freedom. Investors have to thrive even in an atmosphere of constant change. It's challenging because, in many cases, people are using a broken model of investment management. They're either constantly chasing the next hot tip, new issue, or quick-win investment idea to achieve wealth rapidly, or conversely, are stuck in "active inertia," running in circles to improve a stale investment plan that is getting them nowhere fast. We will show how to break through these unhealthy habits by building an investment plan investors have successfully used to minimize losses and maximize gains to exponentially grow their wealth.

The asset mix: a modern approach

A solid investment plan begins with creating a suitable asset mix for the investor. Asset mix is the classification of all assets within a fund or portfolio. Traditionally, assets are assigned to one of the core asset classes: stocks (equities), bonds (fixed income), cash, and real estate. Other nontraditional categories of asset classes include commodities, currencies, hedge funds, infrastructure investments (e.g., bridges, toll roads, airports), and private equity interests. Sometimes, these nontraditional asset classes are called alternative assets.

The asset mix is usually shown as the set of percentages every asset class contributes to the total value of the portfolio. Asset mix is important because research shows that it drives about 90 percent of the variability in portfolio returns. You may recall that in chapter 3 we debunked the "set it and forget it" myth that a 60/40 traditional portfolio was the answer to investing. In reality, in 2007–2008, many investors who thought they would be safe, diversified, and protected from volatility by having a balanced, traditional asset mix of 60 percent stocks and 40 percent bonds still suffered significant losses.

Another equally outdated rule of thumb used to sometimes determine the appropriate asset mix is based on subtracting your age from one hundred; the answer corresponds to how much you would assign to stocks (equities), with the balance going to fixed income (bonds). For example, if you were sixty years old, this rule of thumb would suggest a 40 percent allocation to stocks and 60 percent to bonds. However, this oversimplifies the important asset mix decision, and it fails to take into consideration whether it's a good point in the economic cycle in which to invest in stocks or bonds at all.

We take a different approach to assessing the appropriate asset mix for investors, one that takes into consideration *both* the unique circumstances of the investor *and* the current investment environment. Your unique investor circumstances may include your tolerance for downside risk (i.e., losses), desire for income, time horizon, tax liabilities, and cash flow needs.

The "Stay Wealthy" and "Grow Your Wealth" approaches to asset mix

Let's consider, out of all the money and wealth you have accumulated over the years, how much you would want to keep safe, meaning that it may not increase or decrease much over time. Let's call this portion your "Stay Wealthy" portfolio.

Next, consider how much you would be willing to risk in a portfolio that is designed to grow, participating in the market fluctuations but increasing what you already have over the long term? Let's call this portion your "Grow Your Wealth" portfolio.

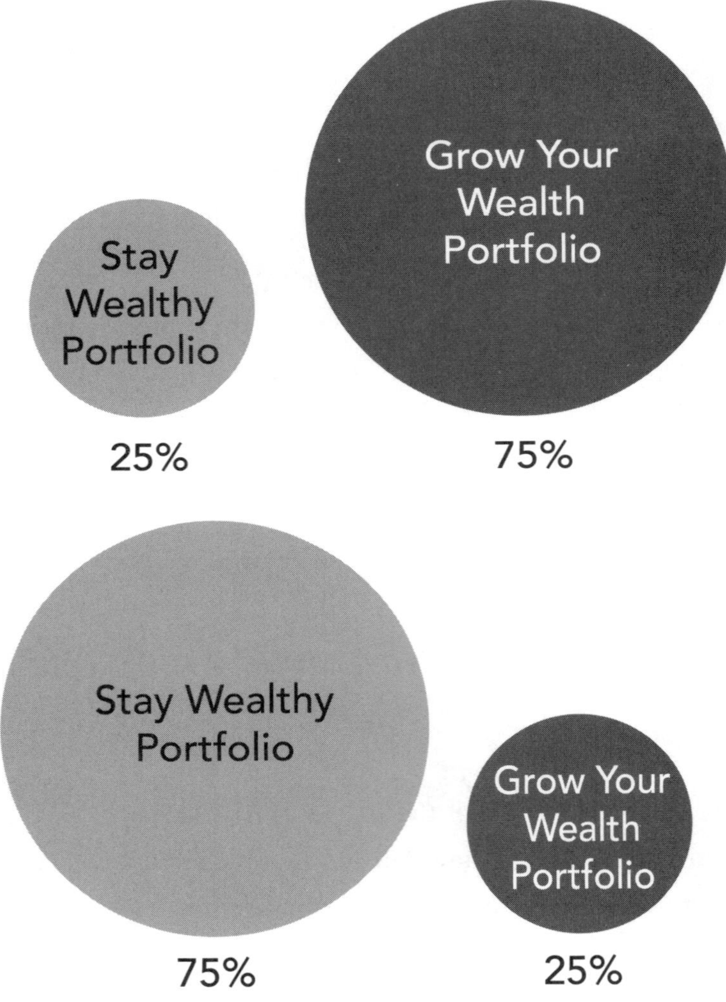

There is an important distinction between the return profile and the risk profile of each portfolio. The "Grow Your Wealth" portfolio could decrease in value and be more volatile than the "Stay Wealthy" portfolio, and that is the trade-off between higher return and higher risk.

Younger clients might choose to allocate just 20 percent in the "Stay Wealthy" portfolio and up to 80 percent in the "Grow Your Wealth" portfolio, as they have a longer time horizon and greater tolerance of risk today in order to capitalize on a higher return over time. Clients in their sixties who are in their active retirement phase still might have only 40 percent in the "Stay Wealthy" portfolio and a majority, 60 percent, in the "Grow Your Wealth" portfolio because they are preparing for the likelihood that they will live longer and wish to sustain their lifestyle. Very wealthy clients, I've found, typically choose to keep about 80 percent of their assets in the "Stay Wealthy" portfolio, as they already have what they need, and their main priority is to keep it that way and preserve their existing capital.

Your Stay Wealthy versus Grow Your Wealth proportions will depend on your *purpose* for the money, which is why we recommend starting with your goals in mind. As we explored in chapter 5, do you want to maintain a Work-Optional Life? Leave a legacy for the next generation or to charity? Or have enough to never outlive your capital and have your last check bounce?

When Victor passed away, Nancy was sixty-eight years old and primarily focused on just sustaining income for her own life. Her greatest fear was outliving her investment capital, the key assets that Victor had left her to generate cash flow for her living expenses. She also had a secondary wish: to grow the value of their estate, to leave something for her sons, daughters-in-law, and grandchildren. So, for Nancy, we structured a mix of 70 percent in the "Stay Wealthy" portfolio of assets and 30 percent in the "Grow Your Wealth" portfolio of assets.

Introducing the "Grow Your Wealth" portfolio

Growing your wealth over time is as much about taking Smart Risks as it's about avoiding the pitfalls and common investor mistakes outlined earlier. So once you have an updated financial plan and you have determined an appropriate asset mix, how do you implement an investment strategy that consistently acts as a catalyst to help your "Grow Your Wealth" portfolio withstand volatility and generate substantial returns over time?

The Wealth Catalyst Investment Process: a formula for financial freedom

The Wealth Catalyst Investment Process™ is a multi-step process designed to help investors make sound investment decisions and adapt to changing market conditions in order to achieve higher returns with lower downside risk. This process is based on the foundation of Smart Risk Investing, by managing the magnitude and probability of wins while minimizing the magnitude and probability of losses to increase your chance of successfully reaching your financial purpose and goals. Most often, I use it to help clients achieve a Work-Optional Life sooner or grow their wealth to leave a more impactful legacy.

My team and I developed this process after many years of working with some of the most successful mentors and professional investors in New York and by gleaning secrets from the ultra-wealthy. This process uses a resilient and results-oriented approach anticipating which investments have the best chance for success. It breaks the investment process into a few repeatable steps that involve quantitative (fact-based review of numerical metrics) and qualitative analysis (human judgment based on experience, research, testing, and refining).

It's both art and science

While the quantitative (or scientific) measures provide objectivity and limit the impact of emotional investing, the Wealth Catalyst Investment Process also requires qualitative (or artistic) elements. The human element is critical just as it is when you're undergoing complex medical surgery, and you want a surgeon with great expertise and the latest technology. It's the combination of the art and science working hand in hand that results in the process being both resilient and adaptable.

The Wealth Catalyst Investment Process

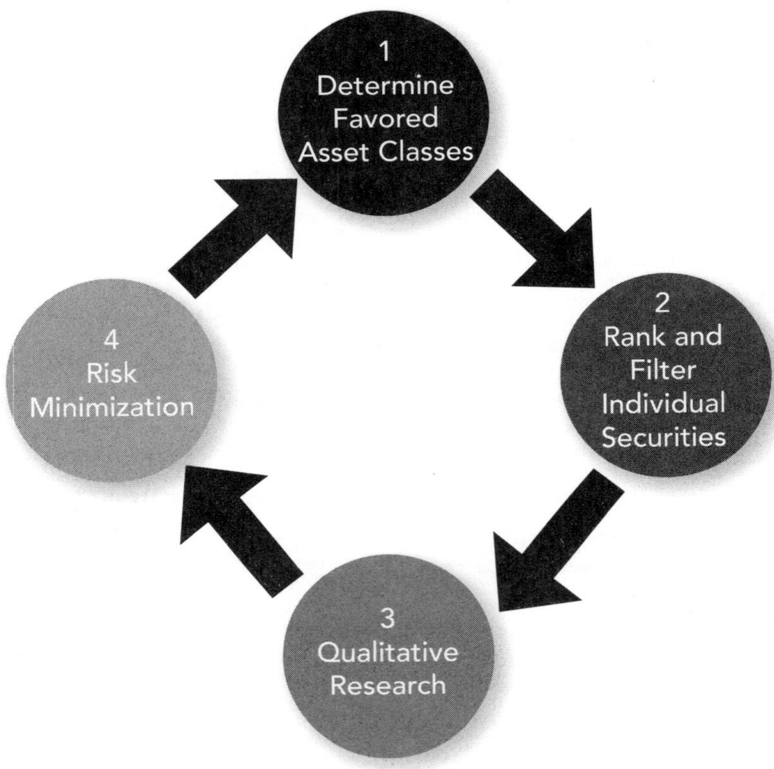

Step one: determine favored asset classes using a big-picture navigation tool

What if there were a way to sift through all the subjective predictions and headline-driven forecasts about which direction the stock, bond, or real estate markets are heading so you could actually identify the most likely future direction of their prices? Instead of being distracted by sensational "noisy" predictions, we begin by studying the relationship between the underlying supply and demand of any eligible investment. This objective step is crucial to understand because the supply and demand relationship is the only pure factor that has a direct relationship with future price action.

The result is an unbiased signal as to which asset class (e.g., US, Canadian or international stocks, bonds, cash, gold, oil, real estate investments, or currencies) are most favoured and which are least favoured to perform well over the next twelve to eighteen months.

How is this done? The heavy lifting work of comparing the risk-versus-reward ratios across securities is done using modern computerized data analytics and software. Asset classes can be computed quite efficiently. This step measures money flows into and out of each security and asset class by recording statistically significant changes in price. The result is a signal revealing the prevailing trend for each security or asset class relative to the other choices at hand, allowing investors to stay with investments that have the odds stacked in their favour, while avoiding investments when the risks versus rewards are unfavourable.

Think of it like a GPS (global positioning system)—in much the same way that a GPS navigates a car driver, it is a tool for the markets that helps navigate the important shifts in trends. A GPS tool is a real-time system that adjusts its recommended path based upon your changing location. When you veer off the path either by mistake or because of a road closure or detour sign, the GPS quickly "recalculates" and suggests the quickest route to get you back on your intended path.

When investing in the "Grow Your Wealth" portfolio, your predetermined path is often in equities or real estate over the longer term in order to exponentially grow your wealth. However, when we approach a roadblock or detour sign, sometimes we need to move off our original path temporarily (e.g., move into bonds, currencies, or cash) as a safety precaution. It is during these times that this first step—called the Big Picture Navigation Tool—in the Wealth Catalyst Investment Process will "recalculate" based on the new data it receives daily from the markets. It then identifies the quickest route (i.e., asset type) to get you back on your path to growth when the likelihood of success is more favourable. Hence, it uses a Smart Risk approach to investing.

It's an objective and valuable step. In early 2008, this Big Picture Navigation Tool gave a clear signal to get out of the Canadian and US stock markets and signaled a shift into bonds and cash. This signal came just months before the global stock market crash in 2008, but it was both a clear and significant signal. After the infamous stock market crash later in that year, many investors who did not heed the signal were left hurt and confused, listening to the tales and predictions of further gloom and doom, and they decided never to invest in equities again. By May 2009, just two months after the bottom of the crash, the signal reversed and firmly suggested buying back into equities, rewarding investors who saw beyond their emotions and followed the signal.

This is an example of how a nontraditional tool that uses a Smart Risk approach can be very useful navigating the shifts in a changing or volatile economic environment. Another way to think of it is as a barometer or a compass to help build a foundation upon which to navigate more effectively and align ourselves with the market. It's also valuable in helping investors avoid losses in asset classes that are most likely to fall.

Step two: the rank and filter approach for finding individual securities

Step two identifies which individual securities (e.g., individual stocks, bonds, real estate investment trusts, or exchange-traded funds) to buy within the favoured asset classes identified in step one. Step two is also fact based, but instead of measuring money flows as in step one, it measures the individual investment based on its quality and fundamental characteristics.

For this step, investors may use computerized screening techniques and modern technology to rank and filter thousands of individual securities based on quality fundamental metrics. Some important metrics to evaluate are ones based on value, profitability, risk, and dividend growth. This step is based on mathematical probabilities and predictable investor behaviour, and thus it works best when applied with consistency and repetition.

One example of a metric this step will rank and filter is *earnings surprise*. When a company fails to meet profit expectations (considered a negative earnings surprise), our analysis has shown that there is a 70 percent chance the company will disappoint again. We believe in the cockroach theory: you rarely see just one. Conversely, those companies that consistently exceed profit expectations (i.e., a positive earnings surprise) tend to continue to beat and outperform their peers, becoming an attractive investment to consider and qualify for the next step in the process.

Overall, step two allows investors to filter out the securities that don't measure up and take only the best-quality securities forward to the next step in the Wealth Catalyst Investment Process.

Step three: the art of qualitative research and analysis

Step three is the interpretation, the art or the human part, where investors can perform further due diligence to get to know the companies and the management teams. We use our professional expertise as a filter to further weed out the securities for the portfolio. For example, if we know that a company is measuring well, based on the first two steps, but that a new threat or change of management may jeopardize its future, then we may pass on investing in that company in favour of another highly ranked investment.

This step is where many years of direct investment analysis experience shines through. Human interjection in the process is important to help balance the art and science of the process and avoid the pitfalls of a purely algorithmic or purely quantitative approach, but it may require professional assistance.

Step four: the risk minimization technique of watering the flowers and pulling the weeds

Managing a portfolio of individual stocks, bonds, real estate investment trusts, exchange traded funds, or other individual securities can be a lot of work, especially today as global markets are more closely linked across many time zones. Thus, it's important to have a process for managing risk in real time, for preventing the unexpected from having a significant negative impact on your portfolio.

Research shows that long-term returns are substantially improved by maintaining winning positions while cutting losses early. The problem is that it's hard, emotionally, to do this. Thus, consider overlaying a risk minimization step that consistently monitors change and signals taking action when necessary. It's a bit like gardening: pulling the weeds (investments that are lagging) and watering the flowers (investment winners) to nurture a healthy portfolio over the long term. And as with gardening, the work is never done. Trim your weakest performers, and use stop losses to prevent any one stock from dropping to hurt the whole portfolio. A stop loss is a decision to sell a security if it reaches a certain price in order to limit losses. This step helps overcome the natural human bias that tends to want to hang on to losers in the portfolio.

This fourth step is useful because when you trim, it allows you to reinvest in companies that rank better. Similar to how the great Warren Buffett continually nourished his best investments and minimized exposure to his losing investments, this Smart Risk Investing approach is about dynamically adapting and consistently making a series of small decisions, each with good probability of success.

Stocks and love do not mix

Let me share an example of this Wealth Catalyst Investment Process at work. We once managed a portfolio that included shares in a successful car dealership business operating across North America. This investment initially met all the first few steps beautifully. At the time of investment a few years ago, the company was making lots of money buying, leasing, and selling cars. It had been earning a 30 percent annual profit growth when we first invested in it, at around $33 per share.

We held the shares as they steadily rose all the way up to about $90 per share, when the company's profit growth began to slow and the company's ranking in our Wealth Catalyst Investment Process began to fall. The shares had done tremendously well, but after following the process through the first four steps, we decided to take action.

So we began to trim the position and sold half of our portfolio's holding of those shares above $80 per share, locking in a profit. In the days that followed, its shares dropped about 10 percent as the rest of the market began to recognize its slowing profit growth, and we subsequently sold the rest of our position at $76 a share. It actually kind of hurt to sell the shares because the investment had done so well and was a good performer, but in following the process, we were able to reinvest the money in something else that had better prospects at that time.

After we sold the shares, the company's share price continued to slide, as it came in line with earlier and lower levels of earnings growth. The shares dropped all the way back below the $30 level within the next year and a half. So had we not taken our risk minimization step, we would have given up all of our gains.

Instead, the Wealth Catalyst Investment Process allowed us to get in and out for our clients at a favourable time. When the shares traded back near $30 a share (the initial level of investment), some clients asked about getting back in. I replied, "I'd be happy to add it back to our portfolio again if it ranks well compared to the other investment opportunities we are reviewing." So it takes the emotion out of getting stuck in a story. We're familiar with the story, but this process ensures that we *do not* fall in love with the stock.

Introducing the "Stay Wealthy" portfolio

The "Stay Wealthy" portfolio provides a solid foundation to an investment plan and consists of financial assets that provide stability and strength across all market conditions but may not keep up with higher-growth assets (i.e., the ones held in the "Grow Your Wealth" portfolio).

What types of investment belong in the "Stay Wealthy" portfolio? The assets that belong in this portfolio might be different from the traditional foundation layer. Traditionally, when searching for low-risk or conservative investments, investors may simply consider bonds or GICs (guaranteed investment certificates) or bank term deposits. However, investors should also consider including other assets such as real estate or even insurance in this portfolio. Life insurance, in particular, can be a great way to grow or replace fixed income assets in a Smart Risk way.

Life insurance in your "Stay Wealthy" portfolio

Consider life insurance as an alternative asset that fits well into a conservative "Stay Wealthy" portfolio. Individuals who qualify can deposit money into a permanent life insurance policy and earn a positive return on a portion of that deposit for growth that is sheltered from tax. The type of product that we often consider to be a Smart Risk investment is a permanent insurance policy. In some permanent insurance policies, the dividend scale (which is similar to a rate of return on the cash value portion) has been averaging 5 percent to 7 percent annually for the past fifty years. This presents a really interesting alternative to traditional fixed income investments because it also provides a tax-free lump sum (referred to as the "death benefit") to your beneficiaries, in addition to the tax-protected growth of the cash value each year. For Nancy, Victor's widow, we established a permanent insurance policy that had many benefits:

- *Diversification*. The financial worth of the cash value and death benefit do not fluctuate in the same manner as other traditional investments and can reduce the overall volatility of your portfolio.
- *Tax-sheltered growth*. The annual growth is not taxed if held until life expectancy.
- *Liquidity*. Owners have access to the cash value while alive.
- *Timing*. A lump sum of cash is paid out precisely when estate taxes are due.
- *Flexibility*. Deposits and payments can be modified.

Structured notes in your "Stay Wealthy" portfolio

Another asset to consider in this foundational portfolio is a structured note, which can provide a guarantee on the capital you have invested while, at the same time, providing you with some upside linked to growth investments. If the markets do well, you get the benefit as the value of your structured note appreciates along with the markets. If the markets do poorly, a principal guaranteed structured note still returns the original sum you invested, at maturity five or six years later. These structured notes come in many versions and are now available at low cost to investors, with the reward-versus-risk ratio in the investor's favour.

Annuities in your "Stay Wealthy" portfolio

Another type of asset, besides bonds and term deposits, that can fit in the "Stay Wealthy" portfolio is an annuity. Annuities pay a fixed amount to the investor for life and can be one tool that helps maximize the amount of cash flow the investor (annuitant) receives and is guaranteed for life. But annuities sometimes get a bad rap because once the annuitant dies, the asset goes with him or her: the annuity company is no longer obliged to make cash payments. However, for a portion of the "Stay Wealthy" portfolio, it may be suitable because, like a fixed pension, this portion of the portfolio guarantees an income for life. Thus, in a tailored investment plan, any portion the investor wishes to leave for beneficiaries can be factored into the other parts of the portfolio.

Consider "alternatives" in your "Stay Wealthy" portfolio

Alternative investments are another tool for investors looking for lower volatility in their portfolios and may also be useful in the "Stay Wealthy" portfolio. Alternative assets may include investments like commodities (e.g., gold, oil, wheat, etc.), managed futures, and infrastructure investments (e.g., investments in bridges, toll roads, and airports). Basically, these investments are designed to earn a positive return while minimizing risk, either by being less affected by stock market volatility or interest rates, or providing a long-term cash flow that is protected from inflation, or providing price movements that actually reduce the overall volatility of a traditional portfolio mix.

Look to the successful pension funds at Ivy League universities like Yale and Harvard, which have been increasing their allocation of alternative assets steadily over the past two decades. On average, these Ivy League universities use 25 percent or more of these alternative investments to manage long-term pensions for their employees, and they've been breaking away from the traditional tools over the years.

What are the benefits? They improve the risk profile of a portfolio. This makes sense for pensions, where the idea is to be able to pay out pension income for a long, long time, essentially in perpetuity. This is similar to what a lot of investors in active retirement are trying to achieve. They're trying to lower downside volatility over the course of a full market cycle (roughly seven to ten years).

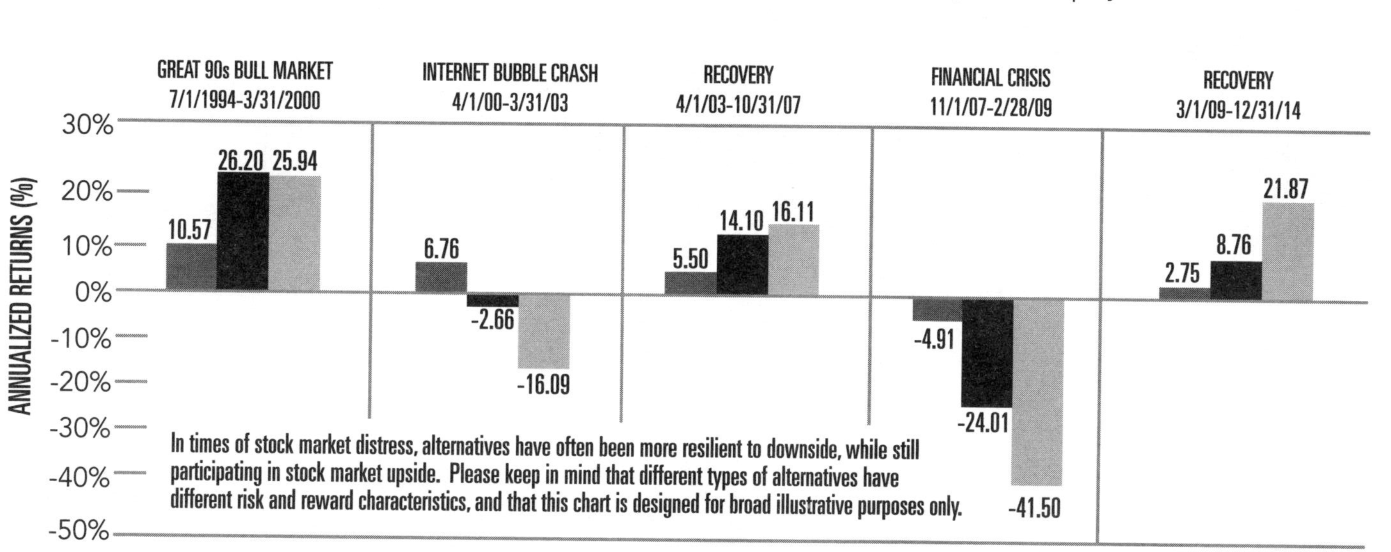

Past performance is no guarantee of future results. Source: Morningstar and Picton Mahoney Asset Management. Market neutral is represented by the HFRI EH: Equity Market Neutral Index. Long/Short Equity is represented by the HFRI Equity Hedge (Total) Index.

The chart on the previous page shows how in times of stock market distress, alternatives have often been more resilient to downside, while still participating in stock market upside. The challenge of using these types of investments is that they are not yet well understood by the investment public, and their accessibility is somewhat limited. But accessibility is increasing and an experienced advisor can help assess the potential risks and rewards on a case-by-case basis. The first step is opening your mind-set to new tools and opportunities and then carefully applying them to your well-crafted investment plan.

Dividend-growing stocks in your "Stay Wealthy" portfolio

Equities can be included in both the "Stay Wealthy" and "Grow Your Wealth" portfolios, depending on the characteristics and risks-versus-returns profile. In particular, investors may consider dividend-paying or dividend-growing stocks as a key component of the "Stay Wealthy" portfolio, for both the steady income and the long-term value appreciation.

Compared to bonds, dividend-growing companies and dividend-paying companies have historically performed well even up to two years after an interest rate hike. In low inflationary environments, basically when interest rates are between 2 percent and 5 percent, returns have been generally favourable for equity markets. This means that the traditional way of thinking that interest rates and stock prices are inversely related isn't always true.

People may *think* they're safer by locking into investments like term deposits when rates go higher, but they could be missing out on significant returns and delaying or never reaching the critical mass of their leaky bucket. In reality, when inflation is under control, a rise in interest rates is often a sign that the economy is getting better, which can favour other assets like stocks or alternatives that may also be appropriate and beneficial in your "Stay Wealthy" portfolio.

Tying it all together

First, design a financial plan around a deep understanding of your short, medium, and long-term goals. Then make sure your asset mix is in the right proportions within your "Stay Wealthy" portfolio and your "Grow Your Wealth" portfolio, aligning with your financial plan goals. Finally, within each category of your asset mix, follow a sound and dynamic investment approach designed to maximize your gains while minimizing your risk of loss. Consider an investment approach like the Wealth Catalyst Investment Process, a multi-step process designed to help you make sound investment decisions and adapt to changing market conditions in order to achieve higher returns with lower downside risk.

Clients who benefitted from planning

Nancy, the surviving spouse of Victor, had an older brother who owned a number of apartment rental units when he suddenly died from a heart attack at age sixty-eight. This brother was a widower when he passed away, so all of his real estate assets became taxable upon his death, as if he had sold them. He had acquired them decades earlier, and their value had appreciated significantly. His two sons, who were his beneficiaries, ended up unexpectedly owing hundreds of thousands of dollars in taxes on the capital gains. It was emotionally distressing for them, especially as they were grieving the loss of their dad. Unfortunately, they had to sell the properties in a hurry to come up with the cash to pay the taxes.

This was the catalyst for Nancy and her own sons. They realized how capital gains taxes could affect them when they saw what had happened to their relatives. At one of the family meetings I hosted with Nancy and her sons, she asked me, "Maili, what can we do so we don't have to go through this same problem?" At the time, Nancy's three sons were working together in a retail business. The business was growing, and Nancy had taken on the bookkeeping to keep herself busy and engaged.

I helped Nancy and her three adult sons devise a plan for their situation, and I put some ideas in place to fill the gaps. First, we recognized the risk to their business and lack of liquidity should one of the sons pass away without protection. The three men were operating at full speed within the business. If something happened to one of them, their wives and their children would be in a tough spot for liquidity because taxes would be due right at the time when they needed money to keep the business running. So we established insurance protection for their business right away.

Next, we built an investment plan tailored for each of the sons. They were each in their forties and were focused on growing their wealth so they could achieve a Work-Optional Life within the next fifteen years. So their priority was investing in their "Grow Your Wealth" portfolios. As their retail business kept growing, the three sons established holding companies, and money accumulated in them. We then started investment plans in each of their holding companies, using our Wealth Catalyst Investment Process approach to grow the sons' wealth.

As those investment assets grew, we began to look at ways to shelter their assets from tax. We worked closely with their accountant and lawyer as part of their circle of trust to make sure that everything was in alignment with the type of tax and legal structures they had set up. The permanent life insurance strategies described in the "Stay Wealthy" portfolio fit perfectly in their corporate accounts and provided true diversification for their business and growth portfolios, tax savings annually and at death, as well as protection and liquidity to pay taxes when needed.

In 2011 their business really took a dip as new competition came in and cut prices. Fortunately, we had anticipated this, and there was some liquidity available in their holding companies from the growth in the investments in their "Grow Your Wealth" portfolios. They were also able to use the cash value in their permanent insurance policies as collateral for loans. As a result of smart financial and investment planning, they already had protection in place, so they did not have to withdraw capital from the business. Their retail company emerged even stronger a year later and has been growing ever since. The success of their investment portfolios allows them to have more options to expand into other areas like real estate development.

Through the years, we were able to help Victor and Nancy's family adapt and shift and fill gaps and prevent exposures just by applying these techniques. We're happy to work with this family across the generations, and their family has introduced us to their friends and families as well. It's been a great success.

SUMMARY

- Getting from the challenge to your financial goal takes resilience and the right plans and people around you to support your journey.
- Financial planning gives you measurable milestones, relevant to your own needs, to gauge whether or not you are on the right track to achieve your goals.
- Investment planning involves the implementation of a strategy designed to build or preserve wealth or earn sustainable income from your financial assets modified for the current investment landscape. What worked as an investment strategy ten years ago may not work today.
- A suitable asset mix will help match your financial plan with the right proportion of risky and less risky assets, of "Stay Wealthy" portfolio assets and "Grow Your Wealth" portfolio assets.
- Alternative assets can complement a traditional portfolio of stocks, bonds, and cash, so you can construct a portfolio with equity-like returns but with lower downside risk.
- The Wealth Catalyst Investment Process is a multi-step process designed to consistently stack the odds of success in your favour and adapts to changing market conditions.

QUESTIONS

1. How well does your current financial plan support your investment plan?
2. What concerns you most about your current investment plan? Is it providing the returns, comfort, confidence, and peace of mind you need and expect?
3. What proportion of your financial assets would you choose to have in your "Stay Wealthy" bucket and/or your "Grow Your Wealth" bucket? In what mix of investments?
4. How closely aligned is your current asset/investment mix to your answer to #3?
5. How is your current investment strategy protected from market volatility, outdated investment tools, and/or emotional decision making?

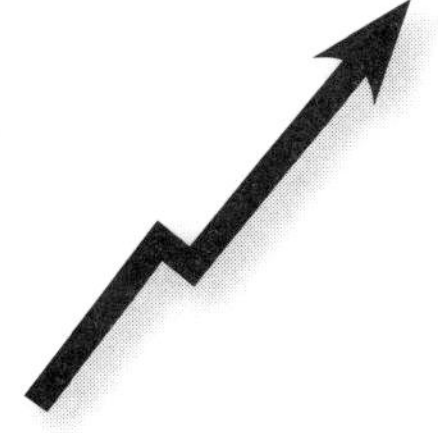

CHAPTER 8

Perspective: What Everyone Can Learn from the Ultra-Wealthy

We can complain because rose bushes have thorns or rejoice because thorn bushes have roses.

—Abraham Lincoln

The Smart Risk Investing Roadmap is most effective when you have the right perspective. The emotional component surrounding money is one of the biggest roadblocks to rational financial thinking. It requires a slight shift in your mind-set to overcome the challenges you face as you build and maintain wealth. Many of these prejudices and opinions are tied to childhood or traumatic experiences we suffered during our lives and now color how we perceive money.

The fear of spending money, for example, is a common mind-set shared by clients who grew up in the Great Depression of the 1930s. This Depression-era mind-set—seeing things dropping in value over time—paints their view of money, whereas, the grandchildren of those clients grew up in a different type of environment and have a totally different view of money (i.e., spend it now; don't worry about debt). These grandchildren grew up in more affluent surroundings and sometimes have a sense of entitlement to money that affects their decisions differently. So changing that mind-set oftentimes is where a lot of work has to done.

But many investors acknowledge their fears and overcome them, clearing the way for their own success. I've learned from working with many of these wealthy clients over the years that success leaves clues. Some people struggle to just keep a job or maintain a long-term relationship or pay off a mortgage, let alone have the ability to save for retirement. Yet, a few have achieved success beyond purely financial measures, building fortunes that could sustain their family for generations.

People operating at the highest level of performance in their life and work, I've found, are not lucky; they're doing something differently from everyone else. And the good news is that even the not-quite-wealthy can learn from the financial management tactics of the very-wealthy. This chapter will introduce the stories of three highly successful, self-made multimillionaires and billionaires who share some uncommon perspectives.

From humble beginnings to ultra success: not your average Joe

I'd like to share the remarkable story of a dear friend whom I respectfully call Uncle Joe. His experience and insights about taking Smart Risks throughout his life have led him to become one of the most successful and wealthy self-made businessmen in North America. Uncle Joe is a prominent member of the Jewish community who was born in Canada, served in the Second World War, then settled in Vancouver and started a retail clothing store business. He was successful, and over the course of about twenty years he started to acquire some large retail stores, and ultimately, sold those to a major Canadian retail company.

In the 1980s Joe orchestrated a $150 million acquisition of a land development company and has continued to be successful in business, real estate, manufacturing, investing, and philanthropy. Uncle Joe's undoubtedly a self-made man, a true entrepreneur. Yet he's never forgotten others; he's always giving back to his community. He still goes to work every day, living a Work-Optional Life. Today, he does not need to go to work for financial reasons, but he does it because he loves it. It's mentally engaging, and he gets joy from continuing to do good work and helping others.

His perspective on life is: "Life is like a bank account, you have to put something in to get something out. You can't take without making deposits otherwise you'll be bankrupt." He really believes that money is only good for what you do with it. He believes that everything in life involves risk. And in his life, it's always been about looking at what he calls the risk-reward ratio. So what is that? Looking at how much reward there is for any given level of risk that he is willing or can afford to take. It's about taking Smart Risks.

For example, some people remark that he's so lucky he paid only $20 million for a building that's now worth over $100 million. But he says it's not luck. At the time he was deciding whether or not to pay $20 million for the building, he was looking at the risk-reward ratio. He realized he could be wrong, and he could lose $10 million. But he recognized that he could afford to take that loss if the bet didn't work. He reasoned that the likelihood of losing that amount was low compared to the likelihood of gaining a much higher amount, so the risk-reward ratio favoured the purchase. In other words, it made sense to Joe from a Smart Risk perspective because the probability of the gain outweighed the risk of the loss. He made a decision to buy the building for $20 million, and it worked out well for him.

But it hasn't always worked out for Uncle Joe. One of the lessons he learned that has helped him along his winding journey to success is the ability to recognize when he's wrong and take corrective action. He says many people are too afraid to admit that they've been wrong, so they'll stay on the same path toward destruction. His perspective supports the Smart Risk Investing Roadmap and the importance of developing an investment philosophy like that of the Wealth Catalyst Investment Process, which is both adaptable and flexible enough to encourage corrective action when things don't work out as planned.

As Uncle Joe puts it, life is like driving down the highway from Vancouver to Las Vegas. You're driving, with your spouse in the front passenger seat, when you come to a fork in the road and you have to decide whether to take Route 1 or 1A. Your spouse says, "Take 1A." And you ask, "Why?" Your spouse says, "Because I said so." And so you take your spouse's advice. But as you drive a few miles down 1A, you realize you'd better pull over to the gas station and ask the service station attendant if you're on the right route.

The service station attendant says, "Yes, this road will get you to Las Vegas, but if you take the other route, it will get you there a couple hours faster." So what do you do? Well, Uncle Joe would get back on the road, make a U-turn, and *take the other route*.

His point is that you make mistakes, but you take corrective action. For example, in 2008, real estate prices were crashing. That was a time when he actually bought six commercial properties. He felt the pain of the falling prices on his other investments, but it didn't hold him back from taking positive action. His ability to see past the emotional fog of fear and uncertainty allowed him to go in and seize the opportunity.

In order to be able to seize those opportunities, he always made sure he had a clean balance sheet. This meant he never took out a mortgage on his own personal home. He would borrow to buy business assets but never at the expense of his personal assets. He said he always paid cash for his home because he always wanted to be in the position to tell the bank to go to hell.

Risk is like betting on horses, he says. There may be six horses in the race: one that has two to one odds of winning and one that's the long-shot. And then there's all the rest. Some people take the perspective of betting on all the horses, which may seem like a guaranteed way to win since at least one of the horses will win the race. But, he says, while that seems to be the safest bet in the short term, it also guarantees you're going to lose money if you repeat that bet in the long term. If you bet on all the horses, in the long term, the house wins because the odds are stacked *against* you. He advises, instead, betting on the horse with the best odds and where the probabilities are in your favour.

Honesty, integrity, diligence, and tolerance: Anthony

The second story is about a dear client named Anthony, a wealthy businessman, real estate developer, and restaurant mogul in Toronto who also started from humble beginnings. He is the eldest of four brothers who came to Canada from Europe with very little. Over the past four decades he has built an empire of real estate construction, hotels, and restaurants throughout Canada, the USA, and Europe. But he does it while keeping a low profile.

He is a friendly and soft-spoken man, but he's known to be tough on those who disappoint him. He demands excellence of his employees. At the same time, he is tolerant of those who simply don't have a similar intellectual ability or business capability, which he understands most people don't. Anthony, now in his late sixties, never makes people feel inferior. He'll modify his speech so they don't feel uncomfortable. He wants people to be comfortable around him so they'll tell him the truth and be honest and up front with him at all times. That's part of his success.

He admits he will put pressure on people who are not trustworthy, but he'll never disrespect them, because he always wants to feel good that he handled things with integrity. He is street smart and a quick learner. He believes that some people are born more capable than others, yet hard work is what really has helped define his success over the years.

Optimism, clarity, and accepting change: Isaac

Meet Isaac. Isaac is in his late sixties and is the quintessential Renaissance man. Throughout his career he has built and sold multiple companies. He's been divorced twice but (fortunately) still maintains wealth both financially and spiritually, which is a feat on its own.

Isaac answers every "How are you?" inquiry with a simple and genuine response: "Perfect." And when he's not consulting for the government or the private sector, he can be found playing golf. He also can be found giving sage advice to one of his four adult children. People can learn from him that it's so important to lose your fear and face all events and circumstances with the simple question: "What is the worst outcome, and can I face it?"

Isaac's other perspective is seeking clarity and never seeking power, because it clouds clarity. And he finds joy in discovery. He believes it's not the end that we should seek; it's all about the process: "Find joy wherever you can and try to be detached from material possessions," he says. "They're good to have when they're not essential to happiness and contentment. And nurture the love in your life. Give unconditionally and you'll always be surprised how much you receive. Don't have any expectations and you'll never be disappointed. Accept that one makes mistakes, but develop the mettle to cut losses dispassionately, never looking back and never getting weighed down with self-criticism and guilt. Nurture optimism."

From an investment standpoint, Isaac's wealth management views fit with a number of our investment theories, including the leaky bucket mentioned earlier. Watch your material consumption. "More is better" is a dangerous, slippery, paradigm slope. And the less you spend, the less you have to earn.

Embracing a Smart Risk perspective and how it helped these ultra-wealthy investors

While each of these men has their unique path to success, they also share some unconventional perspectives that readers may find useful—the perspectives and behaviours that may promote smart wealth building. Below are five characteristics they share:

1. Embracing a Smart Risk perspective

2. Positive perspective and internal state of mind

3. Perspective on failure

4. Perspective on struggling when young

5. Perspective on leaving a legacy

The first common thread among the ultra-wealthy individuals whom I've advised over the years is that they embrace a Smart Risk mind-set, meaning that they actively seek out asymmetric risk versus reward opportunities. They also follow a process of decision making that begins with understanding the trade-offs for each choice, considering the probability and magnitude of each outcome, and finally, comparing those to their tolerance for each before making a decision.

For example, Uncle Joe made many decisions based on the risk-versus-reward ratio. With the $20 million real estate opportunity that turned into $100 million, he initially looked at how much he could lose, realistically, and if he could afford to take that loss. Then he compared that potential loss and the likelihood of losing to the amount of gain that he could eventually achieve and the probability of that gain occurring. Based on his comparison of the risks and rewards, he found the venture to be worth undertaking. This risk-reward ratio (or the asymmetric risk payoff) is fundamental to the process of taking Smart Risks.

Each of these men has also incorporated the key elements of the Smart Risk Investing Roadmap to achieve exponential wealth appreciation. All three of them have achieved a Work-Optional Life and yet still remain active and passionate about the work they choose to do. Let's discuss how the Smart Risk Investing Roadmap helped them so that it may also help you.

Purpose

While he always knew he wanted to be successful, Uncle Joe's purpose for money has changed many times over the years. He told me that early on in life, after he had returned from serving in the Second World War, he fell in love with his wife of now over seventy years. Joe knew her father wanted her to marry a doctor, lawyer, or dentist, and he was a mere emerging businessman. His purpose for money back then was to prove to his family that he could be a worthy husband and provider. He states that everyone's purpose for money may be different. For Uncle Joe today, after his outstanding success, it's not just about making money; it's what you do with it.

People

Some of the things Anthony has attributed to his success include believing in himself and being confident but also hiring others he considers to be smarter than he is. He wholly believes in the value of having the right circle of trust, at every level, from his management team to his professional team of financial, accounting, and legal advisors. Anthony does this so we can enhance his overall success.

In fact, all three of these men work with advisors and surround themselves with teams who think wisely but also differently from what they themselves think. Using a team within their trusted circle allows them to push themselves to perform better and increases their passion for reaching those different goals, including investing.

These advisors help them to see things from a different perspective. This keeps them motivated, increases their resilience to recover from setbacks, and also helps them see challenges as opportunities. It's about having the right team in place.

Plan

All three self-made successes regularly spend time planning and strategizing in their businesses and investments, as opposed to letting things happen. Both Isaac and Anthony were early adopters of our Wealth Catalyst Investment Process, as they appreciated the philosophy of its active yet flexible and adaptive approach, mirroring theirs. Isaac described the importance of having an inquiring and adaptable planning process, "Whatever worked five years ago may not work today," he said, "and it's certain that over the next five years some sort of fundamental alteration will be required. Evolve."

Perspectives

Below are four additional *perspectives* shared by these ultra-wealthy investors that may further promote *positive action* and smart wealth building.

Positive perspective and internal state of mind

Your internal state of mind shapes the way you think about things. It is your mind-set or the natural lens through which you view the world. No one can predict the future, but these highly successful people are willing to see things in a different way. They all recognize they have an optimistic bias, not a pessimistic way of assessing a situation.

Yet when it comes to making a decision, they prepare, measure the opportunity, and respond or adapt in a highly rational manner. For instance, they might prepare themselves to rapidly seize opportunities, as Uncle Joe did in 2008. He waited patiently for that opportunity to purchase several properties. Then when the environment shifted, he took action. It was imperative that he was able to control his own impulses and emotions so he could take the optimal course of action.

Uncle Joe's perspective on life is to always stay positive. He thinks life is too short for anyone to have a negative attitude. He believes negativity is the source of many illnesses; having a negative perspective holds people back. Unfortunate and unexpected things have happened in the lives of all three of these successful people, but they have faced them with positive attitudes. That's something everyone can learn. Prepare for the worst, but be hopeful and positive about the future.

Perspective on failure

Another perspective shared by these ultra-wealthy investors is their ability to overcome their fear of failure. They each will admit they have made many mistakes, yet have built up the resilience and confidence to get up and take a risk again. Building a mind-set of resilience and willingness to tolerate failure in order to keep pursuing success is something everyone can try.

Some think that these people have been extraordinarily lucky, perhaps as beneficiaries of windfall profits or having simply been in the right place at the right time. But in fact, these gentlemen have launched multiple successful businesses throughout their lives and prevailed despite multiple setbacks. So they're doing something consistently right, as opposed to just simply being lucky. That is, they are continually taking risks where the probability of loss is both measurable and affordable and where the size or probability of gain is favourable.

Perspective on struggling when young

Interestingly, all three of these self-made businessmen came from humble beginnings. As my father said to me when I was young, "It's good to struggle when you're young because it gives you much more appreciation for what it takes to earn success, and you know that you can always build it back up again. You just don't want to struggle when you're old."

Uncle Joe agreed that when you're young, you should take lots of risks so you can learn from mistakes and build the resilience to get back up again. Once you get into your fifties or older, he says, it becomes more difficult to recover from these risks. So his advice is to try to learn the pattern of behaviour for taking Smart Risks when you're young, so the positive effects compound over time, and then you won't have to take as many risks later on.

Perspective on philanthropy and leaving a legacy

The Smart Risk Investing Roadmap may have helped these ultra-wealthy investors achieve their Work-Optional Life, but they are now using it to focus on leaving a legacy. Uncle Joe, in particular, is highly generous with his time and resources, but his perspective is that everyone can have a philanthropic mind-set of their own.

Uncle Joe has been tremendously generous. He has written $10 million checks to charities. He has quietly given away money to people who can't meet their rent or have been forced out of their home and have young children or are in an abusive situation and have nowhere else to turn. He's written them checks for the next twelve months of rent. He doesn't tell anybody about it; he just does it because his purpose has become to create a legacy of helping others who need help. He doesn't do it for the recognition or even the tax write-off. He does it because he's in a position to help others in a meaningful way, and he is achieving his purpose by creating his legacy.

SUMMARY

Consider some of these unconventional characteristics and perspectives of the ultra-wealthy that may promote smart wealth building:

- *Embracing a Smart Risk perspective.* Seek asymmetric risk/reward opportunities where the odds are in your favour for a gain.
- *Positive perspective and internal state of mind.* Have an optimistic bias, yet rationally weigh both sides of the decision when taking action.
- *Perspective on failure.* Do not fear failure or rely on luck, but instead, build resilience from past mistakes to systematically work toward success. Take corrective action to limit losses, but do not be afraid to fail and try again.
- *Perspective on struggling when young.* Build resilience early on, when the costs of failure are lower.
- *Perspective on leaving a legacy.* See money as an enabler, not simply a measure of success. Consider a greater purpose, seeking a life of contribution and significance to scale the benefits of your impact exponentially.

QUESTIONS

1. What healthy behaviours or mind-sets are you currently practicing, and how may these be accelerating you toward your desired financial outcomes?

2. What unhealthy behaviours or mind-sets are you currently practicing, and how may these be holding you back?

3. Who do you know who has achieved what you aspire to achieve, and why?

4. Who might be looking to you and your situation as a model for their own success? How can you inspire and motivate others to follow your lead and example?

5. What are some of the common characteristics that you share with these self-made multimillionaires and billionaires? What are some of the differences between their perspectives and your own?

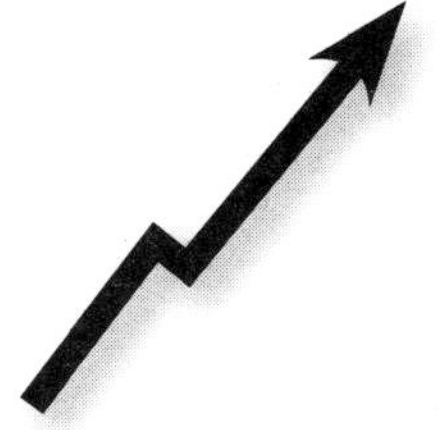

CHAPTER 9

Positive Action: Moving Forward with Momentum

Grit is passionate perseverance of long-term goals, even in the face of frustration and failure. Married with a growth mind-set, it is a potent force for personal progress.
—Philip E. Tetlock and Dan Gardner, authors, *Superforecasting: The Art and Science of Prediction*

With the first four guideposts in place, your Smart Risk Investing Roadmap is fully designed and ready to put into action. You have learned to clear the emotional fog from your investing to rationally and objectively assess probabilities of outcomes. You now have the tools to make choices based on a disciplined, risk-versus-reward process that consistently favours your long-term financial success.

Now, it takes bold, positive action to continue the momentum toward achieving your financial goals. Change can be a scary thing to many people, but the rewards of enacting your Smart Risk Investing Roadmap opens the door to obtain your Work-Optional Life and establish your legacy. In most cases, it's your circle of trust that helps you push your plan into positive action.

Let's see how the entire Smart Risk Investing Roadmap looks—from start to finish—for two very different clients.

You have to look out for yourself

One common obstacle investors must overcome is low expectations of what is needed to afford an active retirement. Many people are living longer thanks to medical technology and better living habits. So the amount of time they spend in this non-working phase of their life is increasing.

Let me share a story about my client Margaret, with whom we applied the Smart Risk Investing Roadmap and Five Ps to overcome her fear of outliving her capital. Margaret is a smart and savvy businesswoman. She is sixty years old, divorced, with an adult son, who lives and works abroad, so she's fully independent. For the last six years while working full-time, she was also taking care of both her parents, now deceased. Her parents lived separately in different towns and required care into their nineties. Margaret realized, as she was taking care of her parents' growing expenses, that she could outlive her retirement savings. She worried about losing her own independence one day and feared relying on her son to move back to North America to look after her.

We worked together to identify the *purpose* for her money and helped Margaret visualize herself in her parents' shoes. She did not want her son to have to help her with basic daily activities. She wanted a way to have additional income if she ended up in a state similar to that of her parents (i.e., living into her nineties, not being able to care for herself, and requiring outside help).

So we developed a *plan* to create a safety net, over and above her existing savings in case her health deteriorated later on. We discussed buying long-term-care insurance, a type of insurance that pays a weekly tax-free benefit to her should she become physically dependent and require assistance with two out of the six basic activities of daily living, comprised of bathing, dressing, eating, toileting, transferring (walking), and continence. If she reached a point in life where she could no longer cope with two of those activities, then she would start receiving a tax-free $2,000 weekly benefit for as long as she needed it.

Considering the option of living benefit insurance like long-term-care insurance or critical illness insurance is particularly important for female clients. Women tend to outlive men and tend to be the caregivers of others. Often their *perspective* is "It won't happen to me." Long-term-care insurance doesn't become a priority until they actually experience a need for long-term care, but by then it's often too late because they're at the age when insurance coverage has become too expensive or they simply no longer qualify on medical grounds.

Critical illness insurance and long-term-care insurance can be useful products for all people to consider as a safety net for the rest of their retirement savings. Critical illness insurance generally pays a lump sum of tax-free insurance money if you suffer from one of over twenty covered illnesses, the most common being heart attack, cancer, and stroke. It provides money when you need it most to spend on getting better or replacing lost income as you recover from such an illness.

Both types of living benefit insurance require medical and financial underwriting and get more expensive with age. Start looking at these options when you are between forty and fifty years of age, or even younger, ideally. Margaret took *positive action* to put this protection in place to preserve her cash flow and independence and to maximize her future choices. Today, after following the Smart Risk Investing Roadmap, she enjoys greater peace of mind knowing that she can remain financially independent throughout her retirement years.

Get out of your own way

Many investors struggle with the obstacle of *inertia* and procrastinate despite mediocre investment results. If you recall, Victor had always been the one in charge of looking after his and Nancy's investments, but for years, he hadn't made a change. Victor and Nancy had very different *purposes* and priorities for their money, but they had not had honest discussions about it.

Involving Nancy in the financial discussions was an important part of the process of overcoming their obstacles. Together, we prioritized their most important financial purpose and goals. First, they wished to secure steady investment income to enjoy an active retirement over the next twenty years, and second, they wanted some growth in their assets to provide a cushion in case they lived longer or required more care. Third, they hoped to leave an inheritance for their three sons and grandchildren.

Plan-wise, Victor and Nancy had none. They were just letting things happen. Prior to our working together, Victor's mind-set was that even though he was losing large amounts of money on speculative junior oil and gas ventures, he believed his advisor would be able to make him big scores eventually. He explained his advisor always had a good story to tell about the stocks he bought him, but really what he ended up holding was a pile of lottery tickets. Most of the ventures were bankrupt, but a few of them were in private holdings, and the market value was way down.

Victor had been reluctant to break away from his existing broker and make any changes. He needed to update the *people* in his circle of trust, and he needed a shift in *perspective*. Victor was holding on to investments because he had paid a much higher price for them and was hoping to sell them once they reached his cost basis. Some of his stocks had sentimental value for him because he had inherited them from his mom.

I helped him shift his perspective so he could see the impact of his excuses and the stories he told himself. Ultimately, the money sitting stagnant was costing him the opportunity to take advantage of other investments. He realized then that his inertia was having a negative impact on his family's finances.

After I walked with Victor and Nancy along the Smart Risk Investing Roadmap, they were finally ready to take *positive action*. They worked with me to update their plans and rebalance their investments—and not a moment too soon. By taking this positive action outside his comfort zone, Victor helped propel Nancy into a more secure and healthy financial situation, even beyond his lifetime. Still today, Nancy treasures this as his legacy.

SUMMARY

- Use the momentum from the first four guideposts of the Smart Risk Investing Roadmap (purpose, people, plan, and perspective) to move past challenges to building wealth and achieving financial freedom.
- Taking action is not always easy and may require several attempts before you build momentum.
- Success is not final, and failure is not fatal. If your purpose is important enough, you will find the courage to continue and not be afraid of asking for help along the way.
- Consider the impact your positive actions will have on the other important people in your life.

QUESTIONS

1. What's holding you back from living a life of undeniable value, impact, and significance?
2. What's holding you back from achieving your own Work-Optional Life?
3. What is one lesson you can teach your children and grandchildren about sound financial habits and responsible financial decision making?
4. Is leaving your family members—and their families—with a sound financial foundation important to you? Why or why not?
5. What is the one step you can take right now to help you move forward and positively influence your family's financial future?

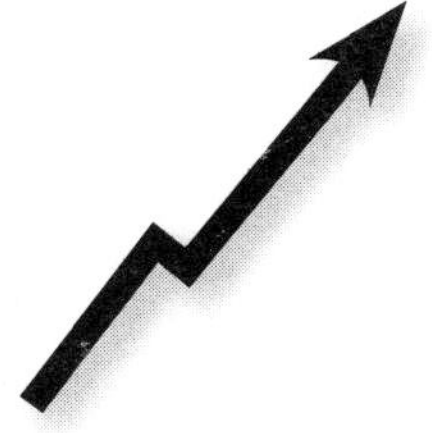

CHAPTER 10

It's Your Turn

Continuous effort, not strength or intelligence,
is the key to unlocking our potential.
—Sir Winston Churchill

The world is a fascinating place to live in right now. And over the next twenty to thirty years it's going to become even more interesting.

Changing technology and the many new disruptive innovations are leading to increased productivity—from self-navigating cars to advanced communication to ultra-fast computing power. These innovations are also greatly improving health care. Medical breakthroughs allow us to overcome diseases and live longer. The onus is on us, even more now, to independently become better prepared to create the income we will need to fully enjoy a longer lifespan.

Yet, too many of us stay mired in a state of inertia or remain too conservatively positioned in our comfort zones. There is an urgent need for a catalytic shift in our thinking that will propel us to build, achieve, or maintain our Work-Optional Life and create the lasting legacy we've always wanted.

Lessons I've learned

My journey, which began in utero when my Mother gave me the chance to fight against the odds, continued as I grew older and resisted the pull toward a life in business, despite having started down the predictable path to a safer, less risky profession. But then the interventions of the Portfolio Management Foundation programme and job offer in New York City caused me to change course, only to find myself, years later, swimming in a new comfort zone on Wall Street in the safety of my prestigious job, financial stability, and independence.

But the tragedy of September 11, 2001, had a major impact on my life as it had on the lives of many others. The impact of living through and surviving that fateful day created ripple-effects that made me question everything: my comfort zone, my purpose, my legacy. Years later, as I gave up everything I had worked for in my New York life, I chose to leap outside that comfort zone and move back to Vancouver to join forces with my father, helping everyday people achieve their financial goals.

And then the global financial crisis of 2007–2008 hit investors everywhere. And my purpose was reborn. Combining everything I had learned in New York with my father's four decades of wisdom, we together embarked on a quest to help our clients overcome obstacles like volatile markets and emotional investing and lead them toward true financial strength and security.

Crossing paths

I feel blessed and grateful to work with wonderful clients from whom I continue to learn every day. We worked with Victor and Nancy to help them first recognize and then overcome the myths and mistakes so many investors make, only to sadly lose Victor too soon in 2013.

Thankfully, we had helped to establish a strong circle of trust around Nancy, including a few of her friends and family, her doctor, lawyer, accountant, and us. So she was well looked after with a strong support network around her, allowing her to find a way forward. We also had established a financial plan, an updated investment plan, and a roadmap for Nancy that seamlessly transitioned to a system that generated sustainable investment income for her on a monthly basis.

We built Nancy a financial safety net, using insurance to give her the peace of mind that she would never outlive her capital. Finally, we helped Nancy gain the confidence to be in control of her own finances by educating her on matters concerning women and wealth through seminars and regular review meetings with me and my team.

Today, Nancy is in a stronger, more deeply rooted place of financial security than she has ever been before, and she is doing it on her own terms with our support. She doesn't even realize it, but she is also an incredible role model, teaching her grandchildren through the positive actions she has taken. She is the real heroine in my story.

Smart risk

Capability is highlighted in times of challenge. Those times when you feel all alone and in despair, much as I did on September 11, 2001, when I felt there was nowhere to run or hide, are the times when the people who truly care reach out a hand to help you. Then you realize you can make it past the emotional fog, and you have the strength to deal with a similar obstacle again, and it gets easier each time. The reality is life is volatile. Life is riddled with risk. There will always be a reason to be scared or fearful about what is around the corner, but you can't let that hold you back forever. Once you are able to come out of that dark, limiting, staying-in-the-comfort-zone place, you can find light, joy, and empowerment on the other side.

The idea of the Smart Risk has influenced my entire life in many ways. It's certainly built into the way our team looks at wealth and investment management. And it's certainly how we help clients move out of their myths and fears toward a better, stable financial place.

Freedom is found in action and not in stability.

Let the Smart Risk Investing Roadmap be your guide

1. *Purpose.* Begin with the end in mind by envisioning your most important goals for the best use of your money.
2. *People.* Seek out advice from experts whom you trust to have your best interests at heart, and be open minded to diversity of thought, as it can lead to better, more resilient

long-term solutions. Building the right circle of trust can save you time, help you make better choices, reduce your stress, and allow you to channel your energy in positive directions.

3. *Plan.* Build a financial plan and execute a sound investment plan that dynamically adapts to your evolving needs and the changing investment landscape. Building these plans together with your spouse or partner can also improve their effectiveness.

4. *Perspective.* Be open-minded to changing your perspective, and consider how the ultra-wealthy have trained their minds to find clarity amid emotional fog.

5. *Positive action.* This next step is what will enable you to achieve your financial goals and, in turn, be a role model for your children, family, friends, and community.

It often comes down to the need for a shift in thinking. This leads to action, putting you in a stronger position and achieving the lifestyle you want. Building resilience, anticipating that nothing stays the same, and having the courage to take action will help you achieve your financial goals. There will always be change. Have the confidence to look change in the eye and take the Smart Risk.

POSITIVE ACTION TIPS

Start investing for a WORK-OPTIONAL LIFE today

Visit www.smartriskinvesting.com to access tools and resources to help you follow the steps in this book toward investing like the wealthy and achieving your financial goals.

Contact the author at:
www.smartriskinvesting.com.

ABOUT THE AUTHOR

Maili is an investment advisor, a portfolio manager and a First Vice President at CIBC Wood Gundy, a leading bank-owned brokerage firm, advising high -net-worth individuals, business owners, professionals, and families. Named Top Forty Under 40 by *Business in Vancouver*, Maili has been recognized as a wealth catalyst for her international clients over the past fifteen years.

Maili called New York City her home for five years, during which she helped manage over $5 billion in assets for Eton Park Capital, an award-winning investment firm spun-off from Goldman Sachs. Prior to that she specialized in derivatives and options at Merrill Lynch headquarters, also in New York City. Maili also worked in Toronto, Canada on the investment team for a global insurance company in 1999.

Maili graduated as "Most Outstanding Female Graduate" from the University of British Columbia with a bachelor degree of commerce in finance with honours. While at UBC, she was chosen to manage a multimillion-dollar endowment portfolio as a member of the Portfolio Management Foundation and simultaneously served as an elected member of the University's Board of Governors.

Maili is a Chartered Financial Analyst® charterholder, CERTIFIED FINANCIAL PLANNER® practitioner, licensed life insurance advisor, and a FAMILY ENTERPRISE ADVISOR™ certificant specializing in helping affluent families transcend their wealth across generations.

Maili lives in Vancouver with her husband, Keith, and their two children, the greatest gifts and joys of her life.

My Vision

- Inspire revolutionary conversations about a new way to think about risk.

My Mission

- To help investors to embrace action – to first think, then act, differently when making financial decisions to achieve their goals and purpose.

My Commitments to Clients

- Be accountable for accurate and thoughtful solutions.
- Be present, focused, and prepared.
- Be a stabilizing force.
- Deliver value efficiently.
- Adhere to processes that support consistency.
- Actively pursue opportunities to grow.
- Advocate to identify and implement resourceful strategies.

My Philosophies

- Capability is highlighted in times of challenge.
- Promises are personal currency.
- Loyalty and hard work are rewarded.
- Money is a mirror.
- Sustainable growth is built on a strong foundation.